Essentials of Employee Counselling

Essentials of Employee Counselling

Fakir M. Sahoo

Ph.D. (Queen's, Canada)
Formerly Professor & Head of the Dept. of Psychology
Centre of Advanced Study in Psychology
Utkal University, Bhubaneswar, India

At present Visiting Professor
XIM University, Bhubaneswar, India

BLACK EAGLE BOOKS
Dublin, USA | BBSR, India

Black Eagle Books
USA address:
7464 Wisdom Lane
Dublin, OH 43016

India address:
E/312, Trident Galaxy, Kalinga Nagar,
Bhubaneswar-751003, Odisha, India

E-mail: info@blackeaglebooks.org
Website: www.blackeaglebooks.org

First International Edition Published by
Black Eagle Books, 2022

ESSENTIALS OF EMPLOYEE COUNSELLING
by **Fakir Mohan Sahoo**

Cover & Interior Design: Ezy's Publication

ISBN- 978-1-64560-308-5 (Paperback)
Library of Congress Control Number: 2022946591

Printed in the United States of America

To students of psychology at Ravenshaw and
Utkal University for providing ignition for professional
elevation during the formative phase of my career.

FMS

CONTENTS

PART 1: BASIC MODELS OF COUNSELLING

Chapter 1: **Introduction**   01
    Employee Counselling
    Scope of Employee Counselling
    Historical Antecedents

Chapter 2: **Psychoanalytic View**   19
    Freud's Approach
    Nature of Instincts
    Structure of Personality
    Defense Mechanisms
    Psychosexual Development
    Theory of Unconscious
    Talk Therapy

Chapter 3: **Neo-Freudians: Adler and Jung**   43
    Alfred Adler
    Terms of the Milieu
    Therapy
    Carl Jung
    The Psyche
    The Collective Unconscious
    Therapy

Chapter 4: **Post-Freudian: Erik Erikson**   60
    Ego and Identity
    Stages of Development

Chapter 5: **Contributions of Post-Freudians**   66
    Horney
    Fromm
    Sullivan
    Rank

Chapter 6: **Behavioural Counselling**   84
    Nature of People
    Principle
    Techniques

Chapter 7:   **Cognitive Restructuring**   92
              Nature of People
              Principle
              Technique
Chapter 8:   **Cognitive Behaviour Therapy**   98
              Donald Meichenbaum
              Changing Client's Self-Verbalization
              Phases of Change Process
              Stress Inoculation Training
              An Evaluation of CBT
Chapter 9:   **Humanistic and Existential Counselling**   103
              Nature of People
              Carl Roger's Approach
              Counselling Technique
              Viktor Frankl
              The Goals of Counselling
Chapter 10:   **Counselling Sessions**   109
              Procedure
              Counselling Memo
Chapter 11:   **Skills in Counselling**   121
              Listening Skills
              Communication
              Interpersonal Relationship
Chapter 12:   **Effective Interviewing Skill**   129
              Attending Skill
              Influencing skills
              Integrating Positive Skills

PART 2: ADDITIONAL TOOLS AND TECHNIQUES

Chapter 13:   **Transactional Analysis**   137
              Structural Components
              Transactions
              Strokes
              Life Positions
              Games Managers Play
Chapter 14:   **Alternative Counselling Models**   149
              The Gestalt Model
              The Reality Model
              The Solution-Focused Brief Counselling Model

Chapter 15: Self-Hypnosis   156
Chapter 16: Avoiding Overthinking   158
Chapter 17: Fighting Fear   163
             The Dynamics
             Fighting Techniques
Chapter 18: Anger Management   168
             The Dynamics
             The Management Strategies
Chapter 19: Managing Self-Control   175
Chapter 20: Planning   179
Chapter 21: Strengthening Work-Life Balance   182
Chapter 22: Managing Oneself   185
             Performing Styles
             Knowing One's Place
             Responsibility
Chapter 23: Management of Pain   192
Chapter 24: Strengthening Spiritual Practice   194
Chapter 25: The Secret of Living Together   197
             Features of Success
             Explanatory Styles

Chapter 26: Train Your Brain   213
             The Dynamics
             Take-Aways
Chapter 27: Management of Thought, Emotion and Time   217
Chapter 28: Meaningfulness in Life   228

Books Authored by F.M. Sahoo

- Cognitive styles and amp; interpersonal behaviour
- Affective sensitivity and amp; cognitive styles
- Psychology in Indian context (Edited)
- Environment and amp; behaviour
- Child rearing and amp; educating assistance manual
- Dynamics of human helplessness
- Sex roles in transition
- Behavioural issues in ageing (Edited)
- Atlas of mind
- Mysteries of mind
- Wonders of mind
- Splendours of mind
- Mind management
- Tools of mind
- Landscape of mind
- Plasticity of mind
- Melody of Minds
- Happiness flows
- Dynamics of Personal Growth
- Essentials of Employee Counselling

Books in Odia

- Bichitra mana
- Manasika bikruti
- Jiban prabahare manasika bikruti
- Adhuni ka jibanare manasika chapa
- Manara manachitra
- Manastatvika bikasare saisaba parba
- Byaktitva & amp; netrutva
- Nari manastatva
- Manastatvika bikasara godhuli parba
- Sisu manara bigyan
- Sachitra mana
- Sabala mana, saphala jibana
- Manastatvika bikasara balya parba
- Manastatvika bikasara kaishore parba
- Manasika samasya O samadhan
- Manara rahasya
- Jibana O' manastatwa
- Tallinata
- Sahitya O' manastatwa
- Chapamukta jeeban
- Sakshyatakara
- Manastatwika bikashar jouban parba
- Sukhanubhutira marmakatha
- Mana Prikrama
- Manara Bhugola

Translation

- Divya Sambasana (Part-v)
- Divya Sambasana (Part-xv)
- Shiridi ru Puttaparti
- Siksha Samparkare
- Bibeka Sampritee
- Chetanadipta Jiban
- Dhyanadipta Jiban

Preface

Counselling is an ever-expanding universe. Since we live in world characterized as volatile, uncertain, complex and ambiguous (VUCA World), pressures are building on our multi-faceted roles. The need for counselling is experienced for parents, teachers, administrators and service-providers.

A prominent sector of counselling service is the organizational context. With an increasing influx of women into our work force, the employees' population presents a formidable challenge. The multi-dimensionality of problems and multi-cultural context of working population the scenarios become further complicated.

Fortunately, the growth of knowledge and multiplication of techniques has offered immense possibilities. The advance of neuroscience has added insights to our remediation process. Counselling principles customized to employees' needs constitute valuable tool box in our immediate surrounding. With the hope of helping management students I have attempted the introductory text. However general readers would also have the benefit of understanding their roles as informal counsellors.

15 August 2022 **F. M. Sahoo**

Chapter 1

Introduction

The American Psychological Association defines counselling as a *helping process.*

> *To help individuals towards overcoming obstacle to their personal growth, wherever these may be encountered, and toward achieving optimum development of their personal resources.*

Counselling is often confused with psychotherapy. Table 1 summarizes these differences.

Table 1.   Components of Counselling and Psychotherapy

Counselling is more for:	Psychotherapy is more for :
1. Clients	1. Patients
2. The less seriously disturbed	2. The more seriously disturbed
3. Personal, social, vocational, educational, and decision-making problems	3. Personality problems
4. Preventive and developmental concerns	4. Remedial concern
5. Educational and non-remedial setting	5. Medical setting
6. Teaching methods	6. Healing methods

Definition

Counselling is a process that involves a relationship between two people who meet so one person can help the other to resolve a problem. One of these two people, by virtue of his or her training, is the *counsellor*, the person receiving, the help is the *client*. The terms counsellor and client, which are viewed by some as dehumanizing, can be replaced by the words such as *helper* and *helpee*.

David Palmer of the Counselling Center at UCLA offers a beautiful definition of counselling:

> *To be listened to*
> *& to be heard ......*
> *to be supported*
> *while you gather your*
> *forces & get your bearings.*
>
> *A fresh look at alternatives*
> *& some new insights;*
> *learning some needed skills.*
>
> *To face your lion-your fear*
> *To come to a decision –*
> *& the courage to act on it*
> *& to take the risks*
> *that living demands*

Employee Counselling

Many firms today realize the importance of attracting and retaining highly skilled, quality employees as a necessary component of their competitive advantage. One of the reasons that a quality workforce along with innovative tools for attracting and retaining has become so important is because previous sources of competitive advantage have become less important overtime.

For example, previously, a firm's success was attributed to an emphasis on product and process technology, access to financial markets, developing economies of scale & learning curves, patents, protected and regulated markets & individual attractiveness. Recently, however, some scholars have noted that these traditional sources of success are less important than in the past and emphasize that the selection and management of a quality workforce has become an increasingly critical factor to organizational success. Today, HR practitioners are busy developing new and innovative tools to attract and retain quality workforce.

One such tool that soon is likely to gain popularity in the corporate world is Employee Counselling. Employee Counselling is a service offered by companies to their employees. Organizations that care for their employees are perceived as more meaningful and purposeful. Every organization has economic and social goals. Here, it is worthwhile to note some observations made by the Chairman of Infosys in this regard. He states, "The task of leadership is to make people believe in themselves, the organization, in the aggressive targets the organization sets. Belief comes from trust: the trust that this organization isn't about making one set of stakeholders better off; it is about making every one of us better off...."

A firm may gain competitive advantages from Employee Counselling activities especially if its reputation and image is valuable, rare and not easily imitated. Employee Counselling therefore is a very powerful tool in the hands of companies in attracting and retaining quality workforce.

Although Counselling is known by many names

like 'therapy' or 'helping' it is by and large, an attempt to encourage change. The counselle's problems could be so complex that it might be difficult to see any system of help as an elegant solution. But, Counselling has shown some effectiveness over the years, as a process of helping people come through with their troubles.

Counselling is a process of helping people to learn how to solve certain interpersonal, emotional and decision problems. Counsellors help their counselles to 'learn'. The criterion for success in any Counselling is real changes in behaviour on the part of the counselle. Counsellors are concerned that their counselles become independent problem solvers. Continued dependence on the counsellor as well as others is discouraged. Counsellors are concerned with habit changes that increase peoples' satisfaction with themselves. It could be anything from helping people choose a career option, becoming appropriately assertive or communicating more harmoniously with team members. Largely, Counselling has been a 'remedial approach'. But recently there has been a slight change in emphasis, from remedial to 'preventive'.

It is rightly said, 'half knowledge is dangerous'. People often harbour myths about the counseling process. Some false beliefs about counseling are as follows: (source: Magazine - Dignity Dialogue, 31July 2001)

No human being is perfect and we all constantly fight our own inadequacies in our own ways. Working in any organization requires an individual to be geared up to face the challenges of work-life. This does not mean he/she can escape the duties and responsibilities of family life, whether married or unmarried. Not every individual is competent enough to take and manage the stress of a hectic life style. Thus, we cannot deny the fact that every individual has intra and inter-personal problems whether at work or at home. The HR function of any organization has the most important challenging job of "making the most" of their Human Resource. Employees can give their best to the organization only if they are in a positive "frame of mind". Mentally preoccupied or troubled individuals will be in a position to give very little to their company

No successful organization will ever be free from stress among its employees. Organization should be able to deal with stress on individuals at all levels. Here the role of Counselling comes in, where people can talk and attempt to solve their personal and work related worries. Need for employee counselling arises due to various causes in addition to stress. These causes include: to deal effectively with one's own emotions, interpersonal problems and lack of team spirit at workplace, inability to meet job demands, over work-load, confrontation with authority, responsibility and accountability, conflicts with superiors, subordinates and management and various family problems, health problems, career problems, etc. Counselling is a process of helping an individual to help himself.

Counselling, basically aims at helping individuals take charge of their lives. For this, individuals need two types of skills: ability to make decisions wisely and altering one's own behaviour to yield desirable consequences. A counsellor's job, then, becomes one of arranging appropriate learning experiences so that people develop these skills. Counsellors avoid giving speeches about what should be done, but ideas for action are developed with the active co-operation of the counselle. The Counsellor does not try to talk the client into feeling that the situation is hopeless. Instead, he/she encourages the client to begin taking action, the successful consequences of which would encourage the client to continue.

According to Eisenberg & Delaney, the aims of counselling are as follows:

1. Understanding self
2. Making impersonal decisions
3. Setting achievable goals which enhance growth
4. Planning in the present to bring about desired future
5. Effective solutions to personal and interpersonal problems.
6. Coping with difficult situations
7. Controlling self-defeating emotions
8. Acquiring effective transaction skills.
9. Acquiring 'positive self-regard' and a sense of optimism about one's own ability to satisfy one's basic needs.

Counselling is discussion of an employee's problem that usually has an emotional content to it, in order to help the employee cope with the situation better. Counselling seeks to improve employee's mental health. People feel comfortable about themselves and about other people and are able to meet the demands of life when they are in good mental health.

Counselling and 'Psychological Counselling' are different from each other. Counselling in the form of advising, consoling and sharing happens in all spheres of life and does not need a specialized counsellor. Even in organizations, this kind of Counselling usually happens at all levels. This is informal or friendly form of Counselling. Psychological Counselling is a process that emphasizes a formal relationship between the counselle and the counselor. The focus of the relationship is achieving specific goals, that is, solving the problems as disclosed by the clients. The help is confined to specific times and days and the relationship ends when the objectives are achieved. The counselor has specialized training and applies the principles of psychology to help clients. There are several institutes, which provide courses in counseling. These courses train postgraduate students of psychology in the specialized field of Counselling. These professionally trained counselors are well equipped to help individuals needing assistance. They are trained to maintain confidentiality, to maintain objectivity and minimize biases or prejudices.

In order to establish a helpful relationship, the counsellor may acquire certain attitudes and certain skills. The set of attitudes required for an efficient counsellor are:

- Respect (i.e.) High esteem for human dignity, recognition of a person's freedom & rights and faith in human potential to grow.
- Sincerity, authenticity.
- Understanding
- Non-judgemental approach towards the counselle.

The set of skills required for an efficient counsellor are:

- Decency skills i.e. social etiquettes, warm manners
- Excellent communication skills which also include non-verbal communication and listening skills
- Objectivity
- Maintaining confidentiality
- Empathy

Through these attitudes and skills, the counsellor creates a positive feeling in the counselle, and a hope that the counsellor will be of some help. The establishment of this rapport marks the start of treatment.

There are seven core techniques given by Rogers, Carkheff and Patterson, which assist the counsellor to apply appropriate core counselling conditions. They are as follows:

- Structuring
- Active Listening
- Silence
- Responding
- Reflection
- Questioning
- Interpretation

Models for human development like mentoring, coaching and counselling are no longer confined to the non-corporate world. These systems are today a part of Human Resource Management of the corporate sector. Inspite of counselling being an upcoming HR system like coaching and mentoring, few companies recognize the significance of Counselling and that their employees will benefit from such a service but may not employ a full time counselor. Awareness need to be created not only at the individual employee level but also at the industry level about Employee Counselling. This is clearly brought out by the primary research conducted by the author herself.

A primary research was carried out in the year 2002 at a manufacturing company based in Mumbai, India. This public limited company has five manufacturing sites across the country and four sales divisions. This research aimed at investigating the (felt) need for employee counseling in the organization. The design of this research study was exploratory in nature. The primary source of data collection was structured interviews, the sample being one hundred and ten (110) employees which is 20 % of the employee strength – five hundred and fifty-three (553) of the corporate office of the company. The interview schedule comprised of both closed and open ended questions. A random sampling technique was used. The employee sample was 20 % of each of the division's operating from the corporate office and was a perfect mix of managerial level employees, staff level employees and worker level employees.

Some important conclusions that were derived from the research study are:

- Majority of the employees of the company (61% of the sample) were unaware of the concept of Employee Counselling. Those employees who had a partially correct idea (25 % of the sample) about employee counseling knew that it was related to helping an employee in distress, advising, creating self-awareness and personality development. The remaining 14 % had an incorrect understanding about the concept.

- After the researcher had explained what employee counselling was all about, 69 % of the sample agreed that there was a (perceived) need for employee counseling in the company. The reasons were many, most common ones being to assist employees solve their personal and/or work related problems and to improve the employee relationships and overall culture of the workplace. Among the 31 % who were of the viewpoint that employee counseling as an institutionalized process was not needed in the company, 57 % of this group felt that the company had a family culture and the informal relationships between the employees could be leveraged upon.

- Only 22 % of the sample disagreed on the importance of employee counseling as a part of HR –systems while 78 % of the employees felt that counseling is an important HR function.

- 83 % of the employees were unaware of the companies practicing Employee Counselling in India (this could also be because the sample was a mix of managerial employees, staff level and workers)

The research results indicate that majority of the sample under study responded positively to the hypothesis i.e. a need for Employee Counselling was felt and that it would benefit the organization. However, the awareness about the concept of counselling and employee counselling, particularly so was found to be exceptionally low.

If a system is being introduced in an organization for the first time, it is advisable to do a pilot. For example, an institutionalized set-up for counseling can be initiated at a particular division/location on an experimentation basis. If this process succeeds overtime, the same model can perhaps be replicated throughout the company. However, for this, the process should be predictable, repeatable and measurable. Some criteria to gauge the impact of employee counseling are feedbacks, dip-stick surveys, focus groups, indirect or direct effect on absenteeism, employee turnover, work performance and productivity, motivation levels of employee's et al.

For introducing and sustaining any new system, the following four steps prove handy – create awareness, educate the employees, then motivate them and finally all this will lead to (expected or required) actions.

1.   Creating awareness:

The starting point to introducing any new system in an organization is creating awareness. Infact in the above mentioned research, 75 % of the sample population was not aware about a trained counsellor in the company (please note the counsellor is not officially designated the position of a 'counsellor' but is occupying some other 'post').

Awareness can be created by various means the most common ones being posters and notice boards.

2. Education:

"The roots of education are bitter, but the fruit is sweet" – Aristotle Educating the employees implies some formal training about the new process to be introduced or leveraging on informal channels. However, a systematic and planned formal approach is usually preferred.

3. Motivation:

After creating awareness and educating the employees, it is imperative to motivate them with the right set of attitudes and values as required for the process. Especially for a process like employee counseling, the mind-set of the employees plays a crucial role in influencing the success or failure.

4. Action:

As is commonly known, actions speak louder than words. If the above three steps are methodically followed, it generally leads to positive results.

Introducing a system is not more challenging than sustaining a newly introduced system. To ensure sustainability of a new system, whether it is employee counseling or any other, the parameters to determine success need to be well defined. For any system to sustain itself, the process should be crystal clear.

The way the corporate sector has opened up to the world economy, it is now high time for organizations to open up for employee-orientated HR processes like counseling, coaching and mentoring. The corporate world is changing and so are the Human Resource Management practices. It is imperative that we adapt the changing styles to manage our people better. It is not just for the benefit of the employees but in the interest of the organization to show that 'we care' about this important segment of our stakeholders.

Scope of Employee Counselling

Historically the term counselling was associated with serious personal problems such as alcohol dependency and marital breakdown. In recent years the term has been widely used in management literature to the extent that some writers have suggested that 'managers cannot avoid acting as counsellors'. However, the term is used in a vague way and often this employee 'counselling' bears little relationship to psychotherapy or other forms of professional counselling.

Performance decline. Managing poor performance is an unpleasant and difficult task and managers do not use disciplinary actions as often as they should; many would rather put up with poor performance than conduct a work performance or disciplinary interview. This lack of desire to manage poor performance is of particular concern as there is evidence that work performance intervention may be the most effective and one of the most important management tasks.

If a manager is to manage performance decline, then performance must be explicitly defined. This requires the establishment of performance standards. Without established performance standards it is impossible to measure any decline. If over time the employee's performance drops significantly from the established standards we have work performance decline. It is important to note that this performance decline should be significant and sustained. All employees may have minor deviation in performance over time due to transient environmental factors, workload or scheduling. As well as established standards, it is equally important that deviations can be measured and observed. This requires properly trained managers and clearly defined and agreed procedures. Most importantly, it requires consistent feedback, rewards when standards are achieved or surpassed, and sanctions when they are not met.

Correcting performance decline. What causes performance decline with a previously functioning employee? Work-related factors such as poorly defined goals, lack of training and lack of effective recognition can affect an employee's work performance. Personal factors such as alcohol dependency, family problems or financial worries can cause employees to lower the quality of their work.

Any diagnosis of the cause of performance decline brings with it the need for action. Appropriate corrective strategies include training, coaching, job design and various forms of employee 'counselling'. The management response to performance decline must address the underlying cause of the problem. If the cause is work-related, the solution lies within the domain of the manager. But what if this cause is a set of complex and private personal problems? Most authors suggest some form of counselling as the appropriate strategy in these situations.

If the manager discovers that the performance problem is caused by personal problems, they are still left with two major problems:

- in many cases the actual causes of personal problems are extremely difficult to diagnose, even for skilled counsellors
- if a manager diagnoses the cause of a personal problem what are they supposed to do (treat,
- refer, ignore)? The solution to this dilemma lies in appropriate work performance intervention.

Appropriate intervention. Appropriate work performance intervention rests on the observational skills (of work performance decline) of managers but there is great danger in assuming that they are able or even willing to take on the counselling role. Their job should be to detect a work performance problem at the earliest time, determine if the cause is work related, and if not offer referral for assistance. This should happen only when two conditions are satisfied:

- the problem must be affecting work performance
- the employee must agree to accept assistance.

The manager should not become involved in private matters; their focus must remain on the work performance of the employee. Problems in an employee's private life that do not affect their work performance are not the business of the employer. There are then three essential requirements for a manager who wishes to conduct an appropriate work performance interview:

The manager should use interviewing techniques to establish if the problem is work related. For example, lack of standards or a lack of training. In these cases the manager should intervene directly.

If the employee's work performance problem is due to personal issues, the manager should keep the focus of their concern on the employee's work performance only. It is important to offer all employees free, independent, professional, voluntary and confidential assistance. The manager must not attempt to 'counsel' the employee about personal problems under any circumstances.

When an employee's personal problems affect their performance or that of the work group, the manager must intervene; referral to professional counselling may be appropriate. Counselling may be offered internally by a professional counsellor or externally, perhaps by an EAP. Some organisations try to get around this by using local community services from a company referral directory. However, this requires the manager to diagnose the employee's problems (e.g. is this employee drug dependent or do they have marital problems?), something they are neither qualified nor entitled to do. In addition, trying to keep such a directory updated is difficult and time consuming.

Historical Antecedents

As discussed in the following sections, counselling typically involves giving assistance. It is done through suggestions and advice. Counselling limits itself to minor adjustment difficulties in living.

The main processes of counselling focus on
1. Change
2. Facilitation
3. Efficiency
4. Sense of Well-being

There are several conditions that indicate the suitability of a person or issue for counselling
1. Help or advice must be sought
2. Must accept need for Counselling
3. Problem must be mild in nature
4. Person is called a client, not a patient
5. Process: one of suggestion / direction / facilitation
6. A minimal level of intelligence is presupposed
7. Client must be free of major pathological problem
8. Injuries / addiction / aging and other biological based conditions out of perview

9. Family based issues may be taken up
10. Main goal is to foster adaptation

The Twentieth Century Development

Traditionally parents, teachers, seers, sages, managers and others have all been giving advice or assistance to people in trouble, over the centuries. These people have provided a variety of psychological and social support to people in difficulty.

However, in the last century certain development provided a clear impetus to the emergence of counselling as a separate discipline. Some of the key factors that contributed to the growth of counselling involve the following:

- Mental Health Movement
- Mental Testing
- Vocational Guidance Movement
- Emergence of Rogerian Counselling Paradigm
- Personnel Educational Development
- Rehabilitation Legislation

The Mental Health Movement. Sigmund Freud identified basic structures of human personality in terms of id, ego, and super-ego. Further, the topography of the mind was expressed in terms of conscious, sub-conscious and the unconscious. More specifically the emphasis on the unconscious underlined the importance of human motives that are latent and hidden. His psycho-analytic orientation paved a new direction for the exploration and analysis of human behaviour. This yielded the concept of intervention in the treatment of difficulties.

The Mental Testing Movement. Developments in mental testing and other forms of human assessment formed the early basis for the technology of counselling practices.

Binet and Simon in France developed and popularized standard intelligence tests. The IQ movement during war periods expanded the scope of counselling activities. Army Alpha and Army Beta (Intelligence) Tests were developed in military setting. Cattell at Columbia University (USA) took the intelligence move further in the United States. A research institute "Educational Testing Service" was set up in Princeton (USA) to coordinate research efforts in this direction. A similar institution National Council of Educational Research and Training (NCERT) was also founded in India.

Vocational Guidance Movement. The evolution of a new psychological speciality, namely counselling psychology, was a remarkable development. Some experts considered it appropriate to assess human ability prior to their entry into schools, colleges, and jobs. Jesse B. Davis developed the practice of vocational counselling for high school students in Detroit. Donald E. Super developed standard for the employment of psychological personnel.

Rogerian Counselling Paradigm. Carl Rogers evolved a counselling paradigm stressing human freedom of choice. His method known as person-centered (or client-centered) counselling emphasized the need for non-directive counselling where solutions were not imposed, rather derived.

Social Service Orientation and Rehabilitation Legislation. The concern for human welfare and legislation protecting the right and interest of the vulnerable highlighted the need for counselling. In organizations, the use of occupational psychologists stressed the requirement.

Current Issues

In today's world, standard of living has gone up. Yet there are problems with respect to *standard of life*. Humans suffer from anxiety, alienation, loneliness and extreme levels of competition. Counsellors are called upon to address the issues of stress, relationship, and happiness.

Besides educational institution and hospitals, counselling offer services in hostels and hotels, sport organizations, health and dietary clinics, old age homes, disability centres, day-care centres, prisons and industries.

The workplace counselling as organizational interventions is expanding its scope. The concept of employee assistance echoes Mayo's (1936) old slogan: a happy worker is a productive worker.

Chapter : 2

Psychoanalytic View

The psychoanalytic view of counselling involves influences stemming from classical Freudian approach, neo-Freudian thoughts and post-Freudian revisions. Sigmund Freud laid the foundation, neo-Freudians (his disciples Adler and Jung) extended the walls of psycho-analysis. Post-Freudians modified the system with the help of cultural meanings and symbols.

Freud's Approach

Psychology in general and psychoanalysis in particular is identified with Sigmund Freud. It is said that humankind has received four blows. Galileo gave the first blow when he shattered the geocentric conception of humankind. Darwin gave the second blow when he said that humans are simply the product of biological evolution. Third blow came from Sigmund Freud who viewed father –daughter relationship being basically sexual in nature. Some people say that Marx gave the fourth blow by explaining human history in terms of conflicts between the haves and have-nots.

Sigmund Freud (1856-1939) was born on May 6th, 1856, in Frieberg, Marovia, at that time northern province of the Austro-Hungarian Empire and today part of the

Czech Republic. Freud was the eldest of eight children and his father was a relatively poor and not very successful wool merchant. When his business failed, Freud's father moved with his wife and children first to Leipzig and then to Vienna, when Freud was four years old. Freud remained in Vienna for the rest of his life.

Sigmund Freud's father married for the first time when he was seventeen and had two children. After he became a widower, he remarried. Not much is known about his second wife. He remarried the third time with a young woman of Sweden, Amelia, whose first child was Sigmund, who was succeeded by seven children.

Freud enjoyed the unrestrained love of his mother who called him "my golden Sigi." This unconditional love prompted him to say "when you were incontestably the favorite child of your mother you keep during your life time this victor feeling, you keep feeling of success, which in reality seldom doesn't fulfill.

Although Freud inherited from his father the sense of humour, his relationship with his father was not easy. Several times he was scolded by his father because he intentionally spoiled his parent's bedroom.

However, Freud's precocious genius was recognized by his family and he was allowed many concessions and favours not permitted to siblings. For example, young Freud was provided with better lighting to rest in the evening and when he was studying noise in the house was kept to a minimum so that he would not be disturbed.

Freud's interests were varied and intense. He showed an early inclination for various intellectual pursuits. Unfortunately, Freud was a victim of nineteenth century anti-semitism, which was obvious and severe in central and Eastern Europe. Specifically, his Jewish birth precluded some career opportunities. Indeed, medicine and law were the only professions open to Vienna Jews. He entered the University of Vienna and completed the medical course work. While at Vienna, Freud also took courses with Franz Brentano, which formed his only formal introduction to nineteenth-century psychology.

Freud married Martha in 1886. In anticipation of Anti-Semitism in academia, he reluctantly decided to begin a private practice. With a meager financial condition, he was able to support his growing family which eventually included six children.

During his hospital training, Freud had worked with anatomical and organic problems of the nervous system. He became friendly with Joseph Breuer (1842-1925). They began to collaborate on several patients with nervous disorders, most notably the famous the case of Anna O., Breuer noticed that certain specific experiences emerged under hypnosis that the patient could not recall while conscious. Her symptoms seemed to be relieved after talking about these experiences under hypnosis. Breuer became convinced that the "talking cure" or "catharsis", involving discussion of unpleasant memories revealed under hypnosis was an effective means of alleviating her symptoms. Unfortunately, Breuer terminated the treatment owing to his domestic problems.

In 1885, Freud received a modest grant that allowed him to go to Paris to study with Charcot for four and a half months. He not only observed Charcot's method of hypnosis but listened to his views on the importance of unresolved sexual problems in the underlying causality of hysteria. When Freud returned to Vienna he gave a report of his collaborative work with Charcot, but it was not well received.

Freud continued his work with Breuer on hypnosis and catharsis, but gradually abandoned the former in favour of the latter. Freud observed that new systems often emerged even though old ones were alleviated through hypnosis. He came to rely on catharsis as a form of treatment. Catharsis involves encouraging patients speak of anything that comes to mind, regardless of how discomforting or embarrassing it might be. This "free association" took place in a relaxed atmosphere, usually achieved by having the patient recline on a couch. Freud reasoned that free association like hypnosis, would allow hidden thoughts and memories to be manifested in consciousness. However, in contrast to hypnosis the patient would be aware of those emerging recollections.

The rich experience and eventful career of Freud led him to a vast empire of ideas. Though the universe of his ideas is really large, major achievements can be summarized under seven rubrics.

The Nature of Instinct

What is the main denominator of human behavior? This fundamental question has prompted all classical theorists to seek solution. Freud is no exception. Accordingly, Freud postulated a theory of instinct. Freud's German word is *Trieb*, for which "drive" is perhaps a better translation than the more common "instinct".

Freud remarked that an "instinct" can be characterized as to three different aspects: its source, its aim and its object. The source is a state of excitation within the body, and its aim is to remove that excitation. The aim is attained in the subject's body through a somatic modification experienced as satisfaction.

He initially offered two major categories- the *ego*

instincts and the *sexual instincts*. Ego instincts were thought to be instrumental for the need of self-preservation. Sex instincts were considered instrumental for the need for the preservation of race (through reproduction).

In Freud's later revision he proposed a new dichotomy: *Eros* and *Thanatos*, the **life and death instincts**, libido and aggression. In this general formulation of his new position, he called upon the science of biology for the support of the idea that there is a tendency in all living things to revert to the inorganic state, i.e., to die. Since all living things arose out of the inanimate the trend towards death may be considered inborn, a death instinct, Thanatos. The striving here is no longer for a "pleasurable" reduction of tension, but towards an absolute zero. Freud accepted for this process a term, the *Nirvana principle*.

With this formulation, the concept of the sexual instinct was broadened. Eros came to represent all the trends in the organism which seek to unify, bind together, preserve and build up. In a way eros included both sex and ego instincts. Preservation of self and preservation of race belonged to the same grouping.

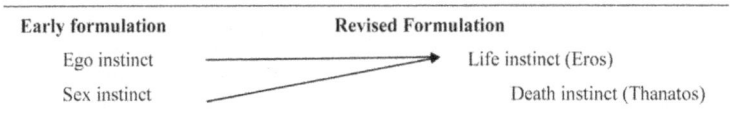

Early formulation	Revised Formulation
Ego instinct	Life instinct (Eros)
Sex instinct	Death instinct (Thanatos)

(Figure1. Theory of Instinct)

(Figure1. Theory of Instinct)

The Structure of Personality

During the early 1920's, Freud concerned himself especially with an aspect of psychodynamics which cross-cuts the concept of instincts. His views have been generally accepted by Freudians. He termed it as *structural approach*. He isolated *three* components: **Id, Ego** and **Superego**. They are thought of as "institutions" or provinces of the mind which become crystallized in the course of experience and there after function with some independent of one another. Of course, they are constantly interactive. After the sixth year, or thereabouts, the latest institution superego is formed.

Related to this structural point of view is the *topographical approach* which cross-cuts the total personality in terms of the various layers of *consciousness*. The id is predominantly unconscious. Because of its biological source, its operating principle is *pleasure principle*. The child is basically id-driven in the beginning. It cares for life that affords pleasure. It puts everything into its mouth. With growing age however it interacts with environment. While putting a pin into its mouth, it experiences pain. Now the child learns that everything doesn't afford pleasure. This leads to the development of ego. Ego does not care for pleasure that endangers life. Thus, reality principle develops.

Exhibit: Three Components of Personality

Source	Component	Operating Principle
Biology	Id	Pleasure Principle
Environment	Ego	Reality Principle
Socialization	Superego	Morality Principle

The perceptual conscious is what we are actually aware of at any given moment. This rather narrow field extends into the preconscious or fore-conscious (the terms are interchangeable), which includes the host of immediate perceptions and memories available to us if our attention requires them.

Perceptual Conscious
Pre Conscious
Ego
Repressed
Unconscious
Id

As I write, I do not hear the street noise- but I can hear them if I focus upon some outside event. The process is quite different with the unconscious. Freud reserves the term for those aspects of our marital experiences which we cannot bring to consciousness when the occasion demands because they are actively *repressed* or otherwise kept at a distance from full awareness.

Superego is the third member of Freud's trichotomy. Originally, all the forces opposing free gratification of biological impulses were lumped together as the censor. Conscience was surely one of those forces. Freud was struck by the fact that the machinations of superego (conscience) sometimes appear quite as irrational and compelling as the id impulses themselves.

Parental dictates become gradually internalized and superego is formed. Initially parents use a lot of do's and don'ts, ought's and ought not's, must and must not's, should and should not's. The child gradually identifies with parents. Their commands and their images become *introjected* – incorporated into the child's own psyche. The child thus, in a manner of speaking becomes the parent and follows the parental admonition as if it came entirely from himself.

Once formed, all the three components tend to operate harmoniously. Freud compared personality to a cart driven by three horses (id, ego and superego). If the horses draw the cart harmoniously, the personality is balanced. If one of the horses over powers the other two, problem arises. Suppose a person is visiting a new house and the host serves a plate of sweets. The id impulse would drive the person to start eating immediately. However, the ego guided by reality principle would sound a signal that one has to start eating only after the guest's verbal request. The request comes and the person starts eating. At a particular point, the superego (conscience) would sound a warning signal "too much sweet is bad for health".

Although Freud has depicted human personality as an interactive system of three institutions, many Neo-Freudians and Post-Freudians have recognized the prominence of the ego (to be discussed later). Investigation of the ego by Post-Freudians has taken an interesting direction of which Freud was the original writer. This involves the concept of the *defense mechanism*. The leader in this direction is Freud's disciple and daughter Anna Freud, whose small volume *The Ego and the Mechanisms of Defense* (1936) remains the clearest exposition of a point of view now very widely accepted among Freudians as indispensable to the work of analysis.

Defense Mechanisms

The concept of defense appeared very early in Freud's writings. During this period, Freud used the concept of **repression** to represent the means whereby instinctual drives are controlled. Later he began the delineation of defense mechanisms. After all, by their very nature, the id materials strive towards expression. But their interruptions into consciousness, either as impulses or as affects, poses threat to the stability of the ego.

How does the ego handle the problem of (a) controlling unacceptable impulses, (b) avoiding the pain of constant conflict and unremitting effort to subdue them, and achieving the harmonious synthesis which is its most mature goal? In 1894 Freud used the term *defense* to refer to the effort of the person to protect against "dangerous" instinctual demands and the conflicts arising in the course of development. Afterwards, he was so impressed by the dynamic power of *repression* that he elaborated other forms of defense.

Repression. The word repression has crept into many paragraphs. Repression means dismissal from consciousness. It should not be confused with voluntary refusal to act upon impulse, often called suppression. When a person counts ten and refrains from punching somebody on the nose, he is controlling his anger, not repressing it. The repressions most emphasized in Freudian theory are deeper. Unable to face the pain of frustration and fears attendant upon expression of erotic wishes, the person denies them altogether. The ego thus excludes large areas of the id from itself- and therefore from the possibility of development under the reality principle. The important repressed materials may include unfulfilled wishes, sexual impulses, fears, anxieties, and frustrations.

Reaction Formation. The power of the repressed impulse is seen in the exaggeration of the tendencies. The man who would not hurt a fly may all of a sudden commit a gory crime. It is quite possible that an unusually tender, sensitive man may give a vicious kick to a cat rubbing his legs. This man is by no means a hypocrite. It is likely that his general life pattern is in the nature of a reaction formation against fears which remain strong precisely because they so rarely are permitted.

Isolation. Isolation is clearly observable in obsessional or compulsive patients. The impulse, thought or act is not denied access to consciousness but it is not permitted normal elaboration in associative connections and in affect. The person keeps the disturbing thoughts segmented so that threat to the ego is averted.

Undoing. A further mechanism found clearly illustrated in compulsion neurotics is *undoing*. Freud remarks that "it is a kind of negative magic in which the individuals second act abrogates or nullifies the first in such a manner that it is as though neither had taken place, where as in reality both have done so." A corrupt person (because of his guilt feeling) tends to show unnecessary kindness to animals by distributing food to animals. A spinster harboring a powerful death wish towards the mother sacrifices herself to the care of this aged mother.

Denial. Denial of reality is a major form of defense mechanism. During a "threatening (frustrating) situation, the person says to himself "none of it has happened". The person denies the happening. The neurotic mother whose child dies may preserve its doll as a symbol or weave the doll into a complicated system of feeling.

Compromise. The technique of compromise implies that the unacceptable impulse is allowed a partial, often a disguised, direct expression but no more.

Displacement. Displacement is a technique whereby impulse is directed not to the powerful object causing frustration, but to an object or person unable to retaliate. An employer in the organization may find it difficult to express anger towards the boss. The displaced anger is directed towards weaker family members "wife and children".

Rationalization. Rationalization is the tendency of

most of us, most of the time, to reinterpret our behavior so that it seems reasonable. The reinterpretation shows us in a favorable light. "Grapes are sour when beyond reach"- this expression captures the essence. Students failing the examination often say examinations are not the indicators of life's success.

Projection. Projection is a technique of attributing one's own faults to others' character. A person who is acutely conscious of his immorality describes others as immoral.

Although defense mechanisms of the ego were not complete, many psychologists attempt to identify major defenses to explore the psychodynamics of individuals. Freud's analysis of the terms of the organism is incomplete with an elaborate description of the genetic process.

Psychosexual Development

Genetic process is one of the most important aspects of Freudian theory, perhaps the most important in differentiating the Freudians from other psychoanalytic schools. With his essentially biological orientation, Freud believed that psychological phenomena should be traced back to their origin in the growth of the organism in its relation with the outside world. Furthermore, this clinical investigation revealed consistently the persistence of infantile materials- unconscious but almost unchanged and very much alive.

Three concepts are basic to the understanding of the genetic process: **stages** of infantile development, **fixation** and **regression**. By virtue of its biological equipment, the child goes through a fairly regular progression. The mouth, the excretory organs and the genital organs successively appear to become the *foci* of psychic energy (libido). These stages may be roughly assigned to age levels much as sitting, creeping and walking. However, there is a considerable amount of individual variation as to the exact date.

The various stages of development naturally show a great deal of overlapping and interaction with one another. *No phase is entirely given up.* Freud uses the simile of an army which, as it advances into new territory, leaves strong garrisons en route serving both the forward supplies and to offer a place of retreat in the event of difficulties ahead. The tendency of the personality to cling one stage of development is **fixation**. The advancing army may come to a halt, digging itself in solidly, sending forth emissaries in disguise or in pretended friendship.

The process of return under adverse circumstances to the point of fixation is called **regression**. The libido retreats. Such regression does not mean that a man of thirty behaves like a child of two. It means that impulses and fears proper to that period regain such power that the weakened ego cannot cope with them in the customary and old fashion but must resort to special devices (symptom formation).

Freud viewed human growth as a sequence of libidinal development. According to Freud, child in the beginning is polymorphously perverted. It wants to derive pleasure from all its organs. Gradually it learns that certain specific zones of the body are pleasure zones and the pleasure zones change systematically with the physiological growth of the child. Because of the parallelism between physical and psychological growth, Freud termed it psychosexual development.

A normal and balanced child successfully moves from one stage to another (deriving pleasure through mouth and then to pleasure through excretory organ). In contrast fixation and regression bring maladjustment in development. The transition can best be illustrated by the specification of characteristics of stages.

The oral stage. The mouth as a pleasure zone is familiar to the most naïve observer of babies. Every mother recognizes the stubborn passionate character of thumb sucking. She is delighted with bubble-blowing oral playfulness of her child. She is also on guard lest this habit of thumb sucking would result in the swallowing of a pin.

Kissing is an important adjunct to genital sexuality in adults. Common sexual perversions involve a substitution of gratification through the mouth for genital satisfaction. The habits of smoking, chewing, nibbling candy and the like testify to the common oral pleasure beyond infancy.

It was Freud who first pointed out systematically the dual function of the mouth as a utilitarian organ satisfying hunger and as a pleasure organ. Freud also showed how the fate of this pleasure drive is bound up with the development of personality. Freud argued that a child requires a requisite amount of satisfaction during each stage. In the event of *under satisfaction* or *over satisfaction* problems emerge in the form of fixation and regression. Although chronological ages change, the child sticks to a particular stage. Thus, a child stuck with the oral stage develops oral personality. He or she may become garrulous or shows some habits like smoking or drinking.

The infant's attitude in the early oral stage is **passive** and **receptive**. When the teeth erupt and the general maturing of the nervous system allows more active mastery stimulation, the child enters upon the oral-sadistic phase, in which the child bites with all his/her strength.

Certainly not all biting at this stage has a definitely sadistic coloring, *but it readily becomes fused with truly aggressive impulses*. Babies come to use their teeth more and more in direct offence or defense or as a punishing response to frustration. By the mechanism of projection, they fear similar aggression in others, mainly in powerful adults. Thus, the primitive experience of devouring can take an aspect of genuine destructiveness. The more the children bite in anger, the more they attribute the same impulse to others. Since oral activity is still the main source of pleasure and its object is genuinely loved, the addition of a sadistic component now makes for a real ambivalence.

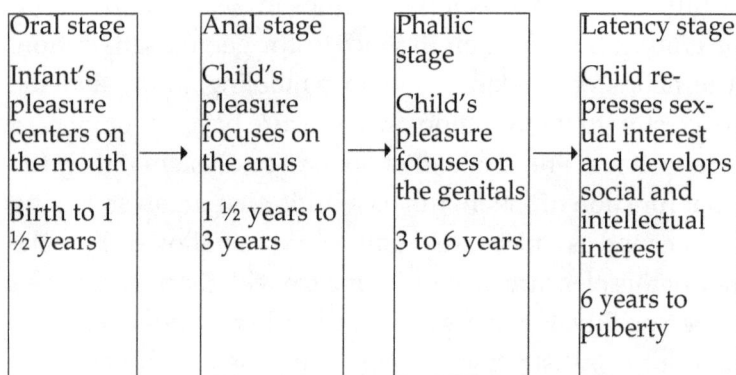

Oral stage	Anal stage	Phallic stage	Latency stage
Infant's pleasure centers on the mouth	Child's pleasure focuses on the anus	Child's pleasure focuses on the genitals	Child re-presses sexual interest and develops social and intellectual interest
Birth to 1 ½ years	1 ½ years to 3 years	3 to 6 years	6 years to puberty

(Freudian Stages)

The Anal Stage. The pleasure aspect of activities connected with the anal zone is difficult for the adult to recognize because it undergoes a much more thorough repression in the course of social development. The neonate defecates passively. Probably the sensation of movement in the aperture is itself pleasurable. At any rate, it seems as though holding in, as well as its opposite, evacuation, is enjoyed for its own sake. Certainly it is in this area that *active mastery of their own impulses* by children makes their vivid debut.

Very young babies typically exhibit a definite, occasionally a marked *cropophilia* until discouraged by their caregivers. They "love dirt", especially their own dirt. Like the object children swallow, it is also part of them. In many primitive societies children are taught to hide their faces because an enemy attack on them would be tantamount to an attack upon the whole person. Unfortunately, anal pleasure *must* be drastically regulated by external demands. Toilet training thus becomes the arena of dramatic conflict among the emerging self-control (ego) of the infant. The manner in which this first conflict is solved easily sets the pattern for the solution of later conflicts. In a broad way the regression and fixation at anal phase leads to the induction of anal personality. Such individuals, in a general way, exhibit extreme forms of stinginess or extreme forms of extravagance.

The Phallic Stage. About the fourth year, the *focus* of individual energy apparently shifts to the genital zone. The child experiences pleasurable sensation in this area. There is fairly continuous growth of sexuality through the partial instincts (oral, anal) to concentration on the organs of reproduction. The sex drive then subsides for a number of years- during the *latency period*- reappearing again at puberty. The early boom of sexuality is called the *phallic* stage to differentiate it from true genitality leading to mature mating and reproduction. At this stage attitude are formed which are crucial for later heterosexual fulfillment and good relation with people in general.

Crucial to the Freudian interpretation is not only the pleasurable excitement associated with the phallus but the value placed by the child, male or female, on the organ itself. This high valuation of the penis is thought to appear spontaneously in both sexes.

The Oedipus Complex. The affinity of the boy with his mother is termed *Oedipus complex*. In the form of demands upon mother's love and attention *generally* this tension between father and son is a matter of very common observation. The term is taken from the Greek tragedy in which Oedipus murders his father and marries his mother. In Greek story, it was prophesized before the birth of the prince that he would kill his father and marry his mother. Hence the king orders to throw the new born baby to the other side of the mountain. The prince survived and grew in the other territory. Gradually he became the king of that territory. In the course of his conquest he crossed the mountain and killed his father without knowing the true relationship. As a conqueror he also married his mother unwittingly. Ultimately he knew and committed suicide.

The criticism has been made that in the old story Oedipus was in the grip of fate and he committed the crime unknowingly so he cannot be held responsible psychologically. Freud argues that every boy is fated to kill his father (in fantasy). However, Freud also argues that it is not always the biological mother the boy loves, it is the woman who has taken the maternal role for the child.

It is called complex because it induces conflict. Even from a sociological point of view, the boy finds that his father is sharing a major part of his mother's time. The close relationship between his mother and father induces elements of resentment towards father.

This is further complicated by *castration fear*. Many parents actually threaten cutting off the penis in an effort to stop the boy's manipulation of his organ. The little boy also hears the threat from other children. The observation of female genitalia is a sort of demonstration that it can be cut off.

Obviously castration fear is very closely bound up with the attitude towards parents. At this stage the parents are conceived of as omnipotent. Gradually the little boy identifies with the father and becomes the father. This leads him towards the resolution of the oedipal conflict.

If the conflict during the phallic stage is not properly resolved people develop *phallic personality*. It reflects extreme form of self-control and orderliness and extreme forms of disorderliness (lack of discipline).

Electra Complex. Just as boys experience ambivalent relationship with parents (attraction towards mother and repulsion towards father at least initially), girl child also experiences similar conflict. Girls experience attraction towards father and repulsion towards mother. Freud viewed that girls experience anxiety owing to the loss of penis. They fantasize that it was there in the beginning and it has been cut off. They blame their mothers for this loss and thus develop repulsion towards mother. Freud terms this as *electra complex*. The term is derived from Greek story where the girl electra persuades her brother to kill her mother because of mother's infidelity.

Briefly stated, Oedipus complex in boys and electra complex in girls represent the basic conflict between instinctual demands and societal standards. The socialization process gradually takes over and most of the children resolve their conflicts. When societal standards are internalized, superego (conscience) takes its form.

The Latency Period. The setting of the Oedipus complex is aided by a biological lessoning of the sexual urge from about the age of six until puberty. The latency period becomes desexualized. The child shows interest in play objects and friends. The child learns to win recognition by producing things.

In sum, Freud's conceptualization of psychosexual development has two major implications. First, a child is polymorphously pervert in the beginning. They derive pleasure from all organs. Gradually they learn to recognize a single organ as a pleasure zone. The pleasure zone shifts in a systematic manner. Depending on its centrality, there are oral, anal, phallic, latency period and adolescence. A balanced child derives requisite amount of pleasure in each zone and makes smooth transition from one phase to another. If there is too much or too less satisfaction, it results in regression and fixation. As a result, the individual shows imbalance in one form or the other.

Exhibit

Problem Stage	Resulting Personality	Behavioral Syndrome
Oral	Oral personality	Excessive use of mouth(smoking, talking), alcoholism
Anal	Anal personality	Stinginess Extravagance
Phallic	Phallic personality	Too orderly or too disorderly Very self-controlled or very uncontrolled

The other implication is derived from the first. Freud believed that the personality of an individual is set by the time the child attains the age of six. Whatever personality changes do take place later, they are minor in nature. Consequently, all the later maladjustments have their roots in childhood experiences.

The Theory of Unconscious

The theory of unconscious is Freud's architectonic structure. It is one of Freud's unique contributions. Natural scientists believe in the concept of *physical determinism*. They hold that there is event without a cause. Similarly, Freud explicated psychic determinism. According to him no behavior is accidental. Every behavior has a cause although we may not be able to know its cause. The cause is hidden.

Freud authored an interesting book "Psychopathology in Everyday Life". He contended that our slip of tongue and slip of pen are not accidental. The reason is in the realm of unconscious. For example, a person may say that he has forgotten to bring his umbrella from his friend's place. Yet Freud hastens to add that this person has an unconscious motive to go to his friend's place again. Thus everyday mistakes are not unintentional.

Our infantile wishes, sexual impulses, fears, anxieties, unfulfilled wishes and forbidden desires get repressed. These repressed materials constitute the realm of unconscious. According to Freud, the unconscious constitute almost ninety percent of our mental province. It is comparable to an ice berg floating on water. Just as only one-tenth of an iceberg remains visible and nine-tenth portion of it stays submerged in water, only a small fraction of our psychic is visible and constitutes our conscious experiment. The major portion of it remains in the form of unconscious.

Figure :

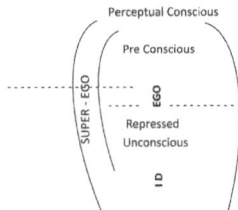

Perceptual Conscious

Pre Conscious

SUPER - EGO

EGO

Repressed Unconscious

ID

Freud clarified how the unconscious operates, not only in disease, but also in many aspects of normal living *The Interpretation of Dreams* (1900) by the most useful and systematic book in this series. Although the unconscious expresses it in many forms, dream is the major revelation. Freud remarked that *dream is the royal road to unconscious.*

Dream Interpretation

The interpretation of dream represents the language of the unconscious. In sleep the conscious mind is relatively inactive, mainly because it is released from its reality testing functions and from immediate responsibility for the execution of its decisions. The motorium is almost entirely excluded from participation in the psychic life; the sensorium is drastically limited. Thus the inward intellective and affective processes have relatively free play without the usual corrective control (censor). Consequently, unconscious wishes find expression.

It should not be thought that the unconscious expresses its wishes openly even in sleep. Very few dreams show their meaning directly. What Freud called "dream of convenience"- as when we dream of refreshing water after a midnight snack of salty food- may also require subtlety of interpretation.

Most wishes are repressed (i.e., become unconscious) because their fulfillment is considered dangerous. Censorship rooted in fear is as sleepless as the wish. The rules of censorship change somewhat in sleep, but they are followed rigidly. If a person dreams too nakedly, he scares himself into waking up. Dream protects the sleep and gives vent to forbidden wishes. Wishes do appear in a disguised form. What we dream is the *manifest content* and what we wish is the *latent content*. The task of the psychoanalyst is to convert the manifest content into latent content. In essence the dream analysist has to crack the code and has to go beyond the symbols to arrive at substance.

Discerning the latent meaning of the dream requires special familiarity with language of the unconscious. Freud suggested some general principles. One general principle is *multiple determinations*.

Several different trends, conscious and unconscious, typically operate simultaneously to determine a given psychic event. The infantile unconscious cannot gain access to any kind of conscious expression unless it can seize upon some currently activated pathway.

One characteristic of the unconscious is it's a logic nature. It means that diametrically opposite meanings stand side by side. It is completely nonlogical. *Freud remarked dreams speak in the language of the illogical.* An important subdivision of the nonlogical quality is its disregard for time. Grief over the death of one's own child may appear in the same dream sequence as the destruction of one's doll at the age of five. Spatial distortion is also found. A big elephant may come out of a small hole. A person finding himself in India may find himself in another continent next moment. In order to facilitate the process of dream interpretation Freud identified a number of mechanisms through which latent contents take disguised (manifest) form.

Displacement, Devaluation, Substitution. The common mechanism is Displacement, devaluation, Substitution. Very often the real focus of the dream is shifted to another aspect or person. A boy nursing his aged ailing father for many months may dream that his employer or teacher is dying. Such displacement protects the sleep and expresses his death wish for his father.

Dramatization. Ideas and affects are very often cast in loose narrative form with mainly visual imagery. For example, a girl saw a lady with gorgeous dresses and magnificent ornaments. She wished and fantasized to have those. Next moment she was conscious of her real position and hence repressed the thought. She had the dream of a marriage party and other elaborate procession. She also dreamed that she was In the marriage procession and she had an umbrella with gold embroidery. Thus the thought of having ornament is elaborated in a different form.

Secondary Elaboration. In secondary elaboration the main repressed thought is dreamed for a very small amount of time, but secondary (nonessential) elements are elaborated. Last example may see golden embroidery for a few seconds, but other irrelevant elaborations may continue for sometime during the dream.

Condensation. The condensation is the reverse process dramatization. A person may spend hours and hours in fantasy. Yet the manifest content may come in a very shortened vision.

Symbolization. Freud observed that symbols of a more or less universal nature are employed by the dreams or other unconscious manifestations. He opined that they must be interpreted as such apart from the particular associations and experiences of the individual. For example, "dawn" as a symbol is conventionalized as "beginning". Although Freud provided a list of symbols and their latent meaning (for example, a stick like object may be a symbolic phallus (penis) or it may be a stick like object of quite special concern to the person.

While interpreting dreams Freud rightly stressed the element of self-consistency. An amateurist may use some catchy example of Freudian examples and may try to interpret someone's dream. But Freud argued that the interpretation derived from dream analyst should be consistent with findings obtained from other psychoanalytic sources (analysis of life events, analysis of everyday errors, projective tests). If dream interpretation is incongruent with other findings the analysis may not be attached importance

Talk Therapy

Pathology and treatment are the medical side of psychoanalysis.

Pathology. It was especially the study of hysteria that gave Freud the first clue to the role of the unconscious in psychic life and suggested the basic nature of sexuality in human development. Freud believed in the idea of *symptom as an adaptive mechanism*. He reportedly emphasized that neurosis results from the *quantitative distribution of energy*, not from the mere existence of a conflict. Conflicts are generated owing to gaps in the balanced developmental periods (birth to six years of age). In essence, all later problems have their roots in the genetic (psychosexual development). The essential feature of the *psychotic* conditions may be stated as the greater depth of regression.

Techniques of Treatment. Psychoanalysis began as a special method of treatment. Freud observed that if the patient lay in a relaxed position and was encouraged to speak out whatever thoughts came to mind, no matter how trivial or shocking the repressed memories tended to come back of themselves. Freud called this technique **free association** where patients *talk out* their problems. The only standard equipment of the analyst's office is the couch, with a chair for the therapist behind the patient. The purpose of this arrangement is maximal relaxation for the patient physically and "socially". Sitting vis-à-vis another person tends to evoke our interpersonal *defectiveness* of thought and feeling. The aim of the free-association technique is to get at the unconscious material with as little interference from controlling and defensive forces.

Apart from free-association a few other techniques are also used. These include interpretation of dreams, the psychopathology of everyday life, emotional concomitants, pattern of reaction, and resistance. As discussed earlier, interpretation of dreams provide information about the unconscious. The analyst consistently observes also small and trivial errors of patient. Coming late or early, forgetting possessions or office items in office, admiring or criticizing characteristics of doctor and the host of small variation supplement free-association in offering cues regarding the unconscious. More recently many analysts are becoming sensitive to physiological cues such as flushing, rigidity or relaxation in posture and changes in timbre of voice. Patients' patterns of reactions are also observed. Probably the most important therapeutic device is the emotional relationship between the analyst and the patient- a device called **transference**. Freud observed that his patients tended to ascribe to him the attributes of God. As the patient *repeats* in his relation with the analyst the infantile relations with his patients

Chapter : 3

Neo-Freudians: Adler and Jung

Alfred Adler

Alfred Adler was born on February 7, 1870 in the suburbs of Vienna. He was the second son and third child of a Jewish grain merchant and his wife. Alfred, did not walk until he was four because he suffered from rickets. At the age of five, he almost died of pneumonia. These events motivated him to become a physician.

In 1895, he received his medical degree from University of Vienna. This is where he met his wife Raissa Epstein. She was an intellectual and social activist from Russia. They married in 1897, had four children, and two became psychiatrists.

He began his medical career as an opthamologist, later switching to general practice. Incidentally his office was located in an amusement park and it was close to a circus site. Most of his clients were circus performers. He studied their unusual strengths and weaknesses. This gave him insights on his organ inferiority theory.

During his youth, Adler was an avid reader. In his adult life, his familiarity with literature, the Bible, psychology and German philosophy made him popular in Viennese society and later as a lecturer throughout the world.

Freud heard about Adler and invited him to

participate in his Wednesday Psychological Society that eventually became a Vienna Psychoanalytic Society. Adler became president and co-editor of one of its journals. Like Carl Jung, Alfred Adler had his own notions. After Freud's discovery that he and Adler were miles apart in their theoretical perspectives, Adler resigned as the president of the group and took 9 associates with him. There were two major differences between Adler and Freud. First, Adler emphasized power rather than sexuality as a central human drive. Second, Adler stressed social environment and deemphasized the unconscious process.

While working on children's organ inferiority Adler found that children with physical handicap in one sense modality were excelling in the use of other organ(s). Adler developed the insight that inferiority experienced in one domain generates a tendency for attaining superiority in other sense modality. Thus, striving for superiority formed a basic corner-stone for Adler's theory.

Adler and his followers became active in the field of education, especially in counseling and teacher training Adler acquired a lot of popularity because of his work, writings and lectures. In 1927, he was appointed lecturer at Columbia University. In 1928, he lectured at the New School for Social Research in New York. Adler left Vienna permanently in 1932 due to the rise of Nazism. He settled in the United States. Adler died in Scotland in 1937, at the age of 67, during a walk after a lecture. He had a massive heart attack.

The Terms of the Milieu

Adler's analysis of environmental influences was largely concerned with the family group. He agreed with Freud on the crucial nature of the early years (up to five / six) in determining personality trends and also on the crucial nature of intrafamily relations. While Freud emphasized biological impulses, Adler stressed the attitude of the parents, especially the mother.

Parent-Child Relationship. Adler's major rubrics are the *spoiled* and the hated child. The spoiled child develops difficulties for two reasons. First, he forms the expectation that he will always be taken care of and his whim is law. Adler found that many criminals were spoiled children. Secondly the spoiled children do not learn techniques of adjustment.

Sibling Relationship. The *oldest* child is the dethroned king. The first born is likely to fight in a variety of ways to regain his lost empire. The second child is in the position of having a pacemaker always before him. The youngest child monopolizes mother's attention. The attitude of the parents, especially of the mother, is a major importance in determining how the problem of sibling rivalry is structured.

Cultural Influences. Adler's official rubrics are focused on the first five years of life within the family. School influence is also recognized.

In theory, a critical feature concerns social participation. Adler eloquently remarks on the high achievements of many underprivileged boys: Lincoln, Carnegie, Jesus. He argued that neither heredity nor environment can be the determining factor. The determining factor is the child's *attitude* towards the handicap of poverty – just as an organ inferiority is not determining in itself but only in relation to what the person feels and does about it.

Adler makes much of the *three problems of life*: social adjustment, work adjustment, and adjustment to love and marriage. Apparently Adler made no attempt to classify social and cultural impacts.

The only exception to this statement concerns his concept of *masculine protest*. Adler denied the existence of any native psychological differences between men and women. Most societies place a premium on masculinity. Girls are made to feel inferior in countless ways. As usual unconscious masculine protent may prompt a girl to exaggerate her femininity or show off her masculinity (polarization effect).

The type of solution hit upon during the extremely malleable years of early childhood tends to orient the person's whole approach to life (his life style). Only in this roundabout way can environmental factors be seen as "causative".

The Dynamics of the Functioning of Personality

The greater the feeling of inferiority the more determined the drive towards superiority. The life style emerges from the initial experience of the child in its striving towards superiority. Adler was among the first to recognize the individual creative, goal-directed structuring behind memory, perception and imagination.

In Adler's writing, social feeling or interest appears as a very important aspect of the child's development, apparently taught by society, especially by the mother. A lack of social feeling in the patient is commonly part of Adlerian diagnosis, and the therapist usually takes steps to remedy this lack.

Fantasy and Dreams. The life style shows itself not only in the pattern of overt behaviour but also in fantasy and imagination in reams and artistic production. According to Adler dream is not merely a combination of the day's residue with repressed infanble wasties, but a *purposeful creation, aimed at integration of immediate problems in terms of the enduring life style.*

If social feeling is weak, fantasy and dream furthers intensify the distance from reality demands. Alder's position is not that fantasy and dreams are bad per se. On the contrary, they become bad only when the life style fundamentally inadequate, since they serve to consolidate personality trends with little correction from reality. Like other experiences, they follow the supreme law: *that the ego's* sense of work shall not be allowed to diminish. Hence the self-deception.

Art productions, night dreams, day dreams, memories elicited outside the pratical requirement of daily living, all have special value for study of the life style, because they are less directly under the control of reality.

Thus Adler, life Freud, considers dream interpretable. He lays great weight on individual meaning, but also offers a lexon for typical dreams. For example, common dreams of falling "indicate that the dreamer is anxious about losing his sense of worth". Naturally the direction of Adlerian interpretation is different from the Freudian.

Adler's emphasis on the *first memory* is unique and deserves special consideration. He routinely asked the patient to report the first thing he could remember from his childhood. Adler believed that such memory is very revealing of the life style.

The Unconscious. Adler rarely uses the term. He explicitly describes the division between conscious and unconscious as an artificial one. His main objection derives from his insistence that the personality functions as a unit.

However, he *operates* constantly with the concept. He remarks that "man knows more than he understands". Infantile wishes, for Adler, are not actively excluded from consciousness because their recognition would entail intolerable anxiety and guilt. They are not simply understood, because of the tight selectiveness of the life style.

Sexuality. Adler totally repudiates the concept of Freudian sexuality. For Adler the Oedipus complex arises out of the dependency of the pampered child on the mother. Similarly the castration complex is the result of the feeling of inferiority. It may be more frequent in societies that place premium on masculinity.

Intrapsychic Conflict. Adler stresses conflict between external environmental conditions and superiority strings. Freud's and Horney's intrapsychic conflict does not surface in Adler's writings.

Anxiety. Adler uses the concept without using the term. It is the fear of confronting a feeling of worthlessness that drives the neurotic into retreat or unrealistic compensation.

Therapy

The key not of Adler's therapy seems to be (1) helping the patient towards understanding of his life style (Adler's equivalent insight), (2) a warmly encouraging attitude on the part of the therapist, (3) help to the patient in finding concrete ways of reorienting himself towards greater social interest, perhaps by a change of situation, more often by a difference attitude towards the situation he is in, plus such outside learning as might help him advance realistically or such outside hobbies as might give him valid satisfaction.

Understanding (insight) meant for Adler understanding of the special devices the person employs for attaining the goal of superiority.

Carl Jung

The Zurich psychiatrist Carl G. Jung (1875-1961)

was among the first to become interested in the new ideas of Sigmund Freud. For some years he was an enthusiastic and favoured participant in the infant psychoanalytic movement. But soon serious idealogical and personal differences developed. In 1912, it resulted in a cleavage. Jung found his own school with a distinct name: **Analytical Psychology**.

Like Freud, many of Jung's ideas were influenced by his childhood experiences. Some of the landmarks in his developmental history demand our attention. Carl Gustav Jung was born July 26, 1875, in the small Swiss village of Kessewil. Carl Jung's childhood name was Karle Gustavll Jung. He was the fourth and the only surviving child of his parents. His father was a pastor in the Swiss church and was poor but his mother belonged to a rich family. His parents started having problems in their married life when Jung was as small as six-month-old. His mother, Emile, claimed that spirits visit her at night and she used to spend her time in her bedroom alone. Though in the daytime Jung used to spend some time with her mother but at night his mother behaved mysteriously. Jung has reported that once he saw a weird headless figure with the head hanging in the air, coming out of his mother's room. His mother was hospitalized for many months for some ailment and Jung lived with Emilie's unmarried sister in Basen and later stayed with his father. The absence of his mother in his early life left an impact on young Jung's attitude towards women. However, in 1879, again the Jung family was reunited.

Jung had described from his childhood that - has two personalities. He described "personality number 1" as living in the ongoing time. He described "personality number 2" as a dignified and authoritative one. These childhood memories impacted his later thought process.

Carl was a rather solitary adolescent, who did not care much for school, and especially could not take competition. He went to boarding schooling in Basel, Switzerland, where he found himself the object of a lot of jealous harassment. He began to use sickness as an excuse. Yet, Carl began a long interest in language and literature – especially ancient literature. He started on Latin when he was six years old. Apart from most modern western European languages, he could read several other languages including Sanskrit, the language of the original Hindu holy books.

Although his first career choice was archeology, he went on to study medicine at the University of Basel. He settled on psychiatry as his career. After graduating he took a position at the Mental Hospital in Zurich under Bleuler an expert on schizophrenia. In 1903, he married Emma. He also taught classes at eh University of Zurich. He invented *word association test* at this time.

As admirer of Freud, he met him in Vienna in 1907. The story goes that after they met, Freud canceled al his appointments for the day, and they talked for 13 hours strait. Such was the impact of the meeting of these two great minds. Freud eventually came to see Jung as the crown prince of psychoanalysis and his heir apparent. But Carl had never been entirely sold on Freud's theory. Their relationship began to cool in 1909, during a trip to America. They were entertaining themselves by analyzing each other's' dreams. However, Freud showed resistance to Jung's efforts at analysis. The distance grew.

World War I was a painful period of self-examination for Jung. After the war, Jung traveled widely, visiting tribal people in Africa, America and India. He began to retreat from public attention after his wife died in 1955. He died on June 6, 1961, in Zurich.

Jung was the originator of some ideas; he also revised many of Freudian concepts. Many of his ideas can be discussed under several rubrics.

The Libido

Jung retains the Freudian term libido but gives it a different meaning. It is more monistic and more pluralistic. It denotes a life energy underlying all natural phenomena. Sexuality is one manifestation of it. It is essentially creative.

For Jung the libido is life itself. As the biological organism matures and as the person has varying reality problems to meet, the libido may follow different channels. Among these channels the sexual (genital) is perhaps the most important. However once differentiation has taken place in the human species, it is inappropriate to consider all libidinal expression as essentially sexual.

Jung suggested three stages of development. Up to the third and fourth year, the infant is concerned with problems of nutrition and growth. This is the stage of suckling. Rhythmic activities associated with suckling become important (hard, for example). It coincides in a general way with the time of the development of the mind and language, turning the child away from parents to the real world.

In the growth of the child it normally moves from the nutrition to the genital zone. The gaining of pleasure leaves the mouth zone and turns to other regions. The possibilities are now many. The libido normally proceeds to other zones, arriving at the genital.

The image of the parents, especially the Mother, plays a crucial role in this development. The child needs nourishing and compassionate figure and fuses this figure with his emergent genital libido. These are prohibited by biological and social fears. The deepest terror the Mother holds the fear of the passivity of suckling era. The image of Terrible Mother, the witch who devours constructive energy appears. Human growth requires a sacrifice of a child self, and rebirth into adulthood.

With the onset of puberty, the child becomes of capable of maturity. The libido (life energy) takes two directions, the one extroversive (outgoing) and the other introversive (inner world). Modes of grasping and forming empirical material are described by four functions: sensation and intuition, feeling and thinking.

The Psyche

Jung's theory divides the psyche into three parts. The first is the **ego**, which he identifies with the conscious mind. Closely related to the **personal unconscious**, which includes anything which is not presently conscious, but can be. The personal unconscious is like most people's understanding of the unconscious in that it includes both memories that are easily brought to mind and those that have been suppressed for some reason. But it does not include the instincts that Freud would have it include.

But then Jung adds the part of the psyche that makes his theory stand out from all others : the **collective unconscious** you could call it your "psychic inheritance". It is the reservoir of our experience in a species a kind of knowledge we are all born with. And yet we can never be directly conscious of it. It influences all of our experiences and behaviours, most especially the emotional ones, but we only know about it indirectly.

The Collective Unconscious

Jung believes that underlying the experience of the individual is the experience of the human race : the collective unconscious. Jung writes: The psychic life is the mind of our ancient ancestors, the way in which they thought and felt, the way in which they conceived of life and the world. The existence of these historical layers is presumably the source of the belief in incarnation and in memories of past lives. As the body is a sort of museum of its phylogenetic history so is the mind. It is only individual ego-consciousness that has forever a new beginning and an early end.

The deposit of the racial past provides a living system of reactions and aptitudes. Jung calls these ancient systems *archetypes*. Archetypes are images which express them in the manner of the meaningful symbol. The archetypes may be distinguished from the more personal symbols. Archetypes belong to the collective unconscious and in this sense transcend the experience of the individual. They do not appear frequently in normal thinking even the thinking of dreams since they are in a way antithetical to the development of ego-consciousness.

Archetypes may be seen in profound religious thought, in enduring literature and art which draw their universal inspiration from the depth of the human psyche. The speech and the art productions of psychotics are deeply revealing, once one tries to understand their basic structure.

Some instances of archetypes may be indicated to specify archetypes. The mother and the various forms she assumes as the life-giver, the all-compassionate, the terrible painsher provide examples. Jung also emphasizes the *anima* (the female counterpart) and the animus (the male counterpart) as principle of the human psychic. This social-image lies deeper in the unconscious. Every man bears within his psyche an *anima*, which represents the feminine aspect of his being. Every woman has her *animus*, the male component.

The soul-image, anima or animus, is the unconscious contra-sexual counterpart of attitudes deeply connected with the orientation of the two sexes: a masculine forming, mastering principle (Logos) and a feminine receptive, loving, nurturing principle (Eros). Both principles are necessary to wholeness of living. The man who too for denies his anima or who too for identifies with it is likely to develop neurotic difficulties. Similarly, the man who too for rejects the counterpart of his attitudinal and functional type get into neurotic problem.

Jung uses the term ego-consciousness for awareness. He has a special word – *the persona* – for the "I" as a product of interpersonal adaptation. The construct of the personality varies in format with the personality type as well as the circumstances of living. The extravert often has several personae, each appropriate to the situation within which he is functioning. The introvert tends to concentrate on one. Although the persona is a necessary and very useful development of the personality, it should not be confused with the personality itself. It is only one aspect.

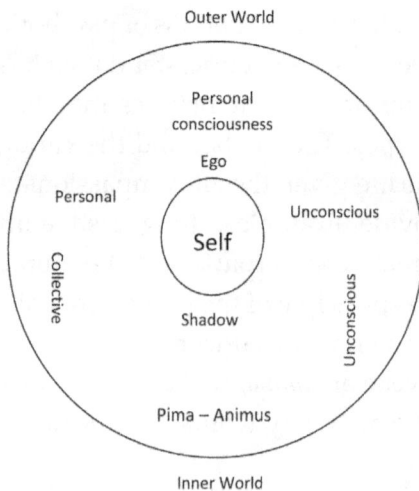

Outer World

Personal
consciousness

Ego

Personal

Unconscious

Self

Collective

Unconscious

Shadow

Pima – Animus

Inner World

The *shadow* represents the unconscious. It is quite literally the shadow, the dark side, the unconscious *obverse* of whatever trends the person has emphasized in his ego-consciousness, in the active trend of his living. It is personalized in the sense that our shadows are related to us as the dark reflection of our conscious efforts. In fact, the shadow may become monostrous and overwhelm the ego-consciousness.

Full development of the personality (of the self) is an adventure and an achievement of heroic proportion, according to Jung. The mass of mankind lives out its span within the safe confines of convention. The hero springs from common human staff, experiences the same needs but he has the courage to go his own way in isolation. It is only by the painful path of conscious individuation, of integration in consciousness of the archaic and the contemporary that the hero arrives at the fulfillment of the human potential.

Mana

Archetypes are not really biological things, like Freud's instincts. They are more spiritual demands. For example, if you dreamt about long thing, Freud might suggest these things represent the phallus and ultimately sex. But long might here a different interpretation. It is curious that in primitive societies, phallic symbols do not usually refer to sex at all. They usually symbolize **mana**, or spiritual power. These symbols would be displayed on occasions when the spirits are being called upon to increase the yield of corn or fish or to heal someone. The connection between the penis and strength, between semen and seed, between fertilization and fertility are understood by most cultures.

Sex and the life instincts in general are represented

somewhere in Jung's system. They are a part of the archetype called the **shadow**. It derives from our prehuman, animal past, when are concerns are limited to survival and reproduction. It is the "dark side" of the ego. Actually, the shadow is amoral – neither good or bad, just like animals. An animal is capable of tender care for its young and vicious killing for food, but it does not choose to do either. It just does what it does. It is "innocent". But from our human perspective, the animal would looks rather brutal, inhuman. Symbols of the shadow include the snake, the dragon, monsters and demons.

The **persona** represents your public image. The word is obviously related to the word person and personality, comes from a Latin word for mask. So persona is the mask you put on before you show yourself to the outside world. At its best, it is just the "good impression" we all wish to present. It can also be the "false impression" we use to manipulate people's opinions and behaviours.

Jung lists a number of archetypes such as circle, cross and **mandala**. A mandala is a drawing that is used in meditation because it tends to draw your attention to the centre.

The Dynamics of the Psyche

Archetypes provide contents of the psyche. Jung explains the operation of the contents with the help of certain principle. The **principle of opposites** suggests that every wish immediately brings its opposite. If you have a good thought, you cannot help but have the opposite bad thought. In order to have a concept of good, you must have a concept of bad. According to Jung it is the opposition that creates the power (or libido) of the psyche. It is like two poles of a battery. It is the contrast that gives energy. A strong contrast gives strong energy, a weak contrast gives weak energy.

The second principle is the **principle of equivalence**. The energy created from the opposition is given to the both sides equally. So, when you hold a baby bird in your hand, there is energy to go ahead and try to help it. But there is an equal amount of energy to go ahead and crush it. How is it solved? It depends on your attitude towards the wish that you didn't fulfill. If you acknowledge it, face it keep it available to the conscious mind, then the energy goes towards a general improvement of your psyche. You grow.

The final principle is the **principle of entropy**. This is the tendency of the oppositions to come together, and so for energy to decrease, over a person's lifetime. In physics, entropy refers to the tendency of all physical systems to "run down" (for all energy to become evenly distributed). If you have heat source in one corner of a room, the whole room will be heated.

When we are young, the opposites tend to be extreme. We also tend to have lots of energy. For example, adolescents tend to exaggerate male-female difference. As we get older, we become more androgynous. The process of rising above our opposites is called the **transcendence**.

The goal of life is to realize the self. The self is an archetype that represents the transcendence of all opposites, so that every aspect of your personality is expressed equally.

Principle of Synchronicity

Synchronicity is the occurrence of two events that are not linked causally, nor linked teleologically. Jung's principle of synchronicity was influenced by the Hindu view of reality. In the Hindu view, our individual egos are like islands in a sea. We look out at the world and each other and think we are separate entities. What we don't see is that we are connected to each other by means of the ocean floor beneath the waters.

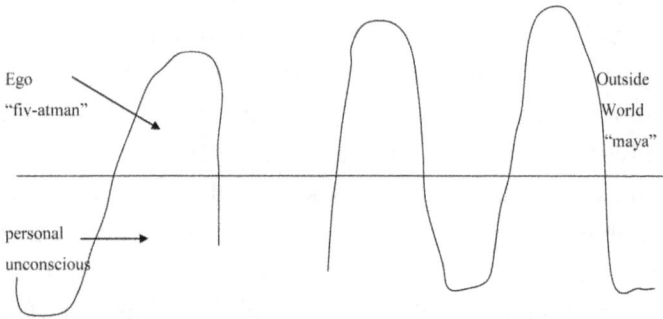

Ego		Outside
"fiv-atman"		World
		"maya"

personal
unconscious

The collective unsconscious or "Atman"

The outer world is called **maya**, meaning illusion, and is thought of as God's dance. That is, God creates it, but it has no reality of its own. Our individual egos (fir-atman) are something of an illusion. We are all actually extension of the once or only **Atman**, or God we tend to forget our true identity. But we never truly are separate when we realize, illusion disappear.

When we dream or meditate we sink into our personal unconscious, coming closer and closer to out true selves, the collective unconscious.

Methods in Psychotherapy

Jung's method in psychotherapy follows to Freud's one. Yet Jung would apply also other methods that guide patients to a personal confrontation with the collective unconscious and its archetypes.

The confrontation aims of the assimilation of archetypal images. In short the individuation as an extensive process that leads to the realization of a psychic wholeness. This includes the conjunction of the conscious and the unconscious.

The main methods of Jungian therapy include *Free Association Test*, dream analysis, active imagination and symbol analysis. In free association test, the patient is asked to answer to the induced words pronounced by the therapist with any word that comes to his or her mind. The response time can be an indicator of the activated unconscious complexes. Since Jung regards dream as a *compensation* to the one-sided individual ego, retrospective interpretation reveals the psychic wholeness. Similarly, the fantasies are considered products of the unconscious, Jung suggested the free flow of fantasies with a view to integrating them into the conscious.

According to Jung, full development of the personality is an adventure. The mass of mankind lives out its span within the safe confines of convention. We have no reason to be satisfied with our current convention. The hero springs from common human stuff, experiences the same needs, but he/she has the courage to go his/her own way in isolation, to be faithful to the law of his being – which includes the dark forces of the shadow and the collective unconscious. It is only by the painful process of conscious individuation of integration in consciousness of the archaic and the contemporary, of the natural bent and its shadow, that the hero arrives at the fulfillment of the human potential.

Chapter : 4

Post-Freudians: Erik Erikson

Horney, Fromme, Sullivan, Rank and Erikson constitute the group of Post-Freudians. Each of them presented separate view of psychoanalysis. Yet, all of them can be included in the label of cultural school. The following exhibit shows a list of concept stressed by them

Post – Freudians (The cultural School)

Horney
- Self-Concept

Fromme
- Self-Acceptance

Sullivan
- Social Relation

Rank
- The Will Power

However, Erik Erikson's contribution requires explication.

Erik Homberger Erikson (1902-1994) was born near Frankfurt Germany, to Danish parents. Before he was born his parents separated, and his mother left Denmark to live in Germany. When Erik became ill at age 3, his mother took him to a pediatrician named Homberger. She fell in love with the man, married him and renamed Erik after his new stepfather.

Erik attended primary school from ages 6 to 10 and then the gymnasium (high school) from ages 11 to 18. There he studied art and a number of languages rather than sciences. Erik's dislike for formal schooling was reflected in his grades. Rather than go to college, at ages 18 he began wondering around Europe, recording his experiences in a diary. After a year of travel, he returned to Germany and enrolled in an art school but became dissatisfied and enrolled in another.

Erik was not trained by Sigmund Freud, nor did he hold a Doctorate from a highly respected University. In fact, he was not formally educated like the vast majority of his psychodynamic colleagues. Although his parents pushed him for medical school, Erikson saw himself as an artist and spent his youth wandering through Europe living the artist's life.

In 1927, he took a job working with children of Freud's patients and friends. The school approached development psychoanalytically and Erikson was soon to master this theory and begin developing his own theories relating to personality development.

The Ego and Identity

Erikson believed that the ego Freud described was far more than just a mediator between the superego and the id. He saw the ego as a positive driving force in human development and personality. As such he believed the ego's main job was to establish and maintain a sense of identity. A person with a strong sense of identity is one who knows where he/she is in life, has accepted this positions and has workable goals and growth. He/she has a sense of uniqueness while also having a sense of belonging and wholeness.

Those who have weaker egos encounter trying times, or who have poorly developed egos get trapped in what is termed as *identity crisis*. According to Erikson an identity crisis is a time in person's life when they lack direction, feel unproductive, and do not feel a strong sense of identity. He believed that we all have identity crises at one time or another in our lives and that these crises do not necessarily represent a negative but can be a drive force toward positive resolution.

Stages of Psychosocial Development

Like Freud and many others, Erikson maintained that personality development occurs in a predetermined order. Instead of focusing on sexual development, he was interested in how children socialize and how this affects their sense of self. He saw personality as developing throughout the lifetime and looked at identity crises at the focal point for each stage of human development.

He conceptualized eight distinct stages, each with two possible outcomes. According to the theory, successful completion of each stage results in a healthy personality and successful interactions with others. Failure to successfully complete a stage can result in a reduced ability to complete further stages and therefore a more unhealthy personality and sense of self. These stages however can be resolved successfully at a later time.

Stage 1 : Trust versus Mistrust. From age's birth to one year, children begin to learn the ability to trust others based upon the consistency of their caregivers. If trust develops successfully, the child gains confidence and security in the world around him / her and is able to feel secure even when threatened. Unsuccessful competition of this stage can result in an ability to trust and therefore a sense of fear about the inconsistent world. It may result in anxiety, heightened insecurities and an over feeling of mistrust in the world around them.

Stage 2 : Autonomy versus Shame and Doubt. Between the ages of one and three, children begin to assert their independence, by walking away from their mother, picking which toy to play with and making choices about what they like to wear, to eat, etc. If children in this stage are encouraged and supported in their increased independence, they become more confident and secure in their ability to survive in the world. If children are criticized, overly controlled, or not given the opportunity to assert themselves, they begin to feel inadequate in their ability to survive, and may then become overly dependent upon others, lack of self-esteem, and feel a sense of shame or doubt in their own abilities.

Stage 3 : Initiative versus Guilt. Around age three and continuing to age six, children assert themselves more frequently. They begin to plan activities, make up games, and initiate activity with others. If given this opportunity, children develop a sense of initiative and feel secure in their ability to lead others and make decisions. Conversely, if this tendency is discouraged children develop a sense of guilt. They may feel like a nuisance to others and will therefore remain followers, lacking in self-initiative.

Stage 4 : Industry versus Inferiority. From age six years to puberty children begin to develop a sense of pride in their accomplishments. They initiate projects, see them through completion, and feel good about what they have achieved. During this time, teachers play an increased role in the child's development. If children are encouraged and reinforced for their initiatives, they begin to feel industrious and feel confident in their ability to achieve goals. If the initiative is not encouraged, then the child begins to feel inferior, doubting his/her own abilities and therefore may not reach his/her potential.

Stage 5 : Identity versus Role Confusion. During adolescence the transition from childhood to adulthood is most important. Children are becoming more independently, and begin to look at the future in terms of career, relationships, families, housing, etc. During this period, they explore possibilities and begin to form their own identity based upon the outcome of their expectations. This sense of who they are can be hindered, which results in a sense of confusion ("I don't know what I want to be when I grow up") about themselves and their role in the world.

Stage 6 : Identity versus Isolation. Occurring in young adulthood, we begin to share ourselves more intimately with others. We explore relationships leading forward long-term commitments with some one other than a family member. Successful completion can lead to comfortable relationship and a sense of commitment, safety, and care within a relationship. Avoiding intimacy, fearing commitment and relationships can lead to isolation, loneliness and sometimes depression.

Stage 7 : Generativity versus Stagnation. During middle adulthood, we establish our careers, settle down within a relationship, begin our own families and develop a sense of being a part of the bigger picture. We give back to society through raising our children, being productive at work, and becoming involved in community activities and organizations. By failing to achieve these objectives, we become stagnant and feel unproductive.

Stage 8 : Ego Integrity versus Despair. As we grow older and become senior citizens, we tend to slow down our productivity and explore life as a retired person. It is during this time we contemplate our accomplishments and are able to develop if we see ourselves as leading a successful life. If we see our lives as unproductive, feel guilt about our pasts, or we feel that we did not accomplish our life goals, we become dissatisfied with life and develop despair, often leading to depression and hopelessness.

Erikson's Psychosocial Development

Stage	Period	Conflict
I	Infancy	Trust vrs. Mistrust
II	Early Childhood	Autonomy vrs. Shame & Doubt
III	Mid-Childhood	Initiative vrs. Guilt
IV	Pre adolescence	Industry vrs. Inferiority
V	Adolescence	Identity vrs. Role confusion
VI	Pre adulthood	Intimacy vrs. Isolation
VII	Adulthood	Generativity vrs. Stagnation
VIII	Late adulthood	Integrity vrs. Despair

Implications Derived

From Neo-Freudians & Post Freudians
1.   Use of self-awareness and self-acceptance
2.   Role of Socio-cultural context

Chapter : 5

Contributions of Post-Freudians

Karen Horney

Karen Horney was born in Germany on September 16, 1885. She dealt with depression very early in life. She described her father as a strict disciplinarian and was very close to her brother, Berndt. When he distanced himself from her, she became depressed.

Horney devoted herself to school, believing that, "I could not be pretty, I decided I would be smart". She began medical school in 1906 and married a law student named Oscar Horney in 1909. The death of her mother and then her brother in 1911 and 1923 were extremely difficult for Horney. In 1926, she left her husband and moved to the United States with her three daughters. It was here that she became friends with other prominent intellectuals and developed her theories on psychology. In 1942, she published the famous book **self-analysis**. She died on December 4, 1952.

Karen Horney's approach is less "pessimistic" than Freud's. She feels that man has the capacity as well as the desire to develop his potentialities and become a decent human being ... that man can change and go on changing as long as he lives". This belief does not mean man is essentially good. It means that man strives towards self-realization and his set of values evolves from such strivings.

The qualities of the decent human being, the normal

personal, is termed *the real self*. Its obverse is the "neurotic" trends in man. The neurotic person is more rigidly, more compulsively, set in his modes of reaction and less able to perceive the "real" demands of the situation. It is decent and normal to stand up for one's rights. The "neurotic" may fight for his rights when they are in no way threatened, or may submissively tolerate an undue amount of injustice. His reactions are determined by his own "neurotic" needs, most unconscious.

The mainspring of neurotic manifestation is seen as a *basic anxiety*. Horney means that a child feels isolated and helpless in a potentially hostile would Horney's emphasis on the helplessness of the infant as a determining factor is similar to Adler's. Yet her position differs from his in two essential ways.

First, Adler feels that because of his initial helplessness very infant feels inferior. In consequence, striving to overcome this normal feeling becomes the guiding principle of all human activity. Horney's position is broader and more cautious. The infant does not *necessarily* feel helplessness in a hostile world. He has multiform capacities for achievement. Has helplessness is seen as a primary condition for neurotic development when actual difficulties in his surroundings make the outside world seem frustrating.

Second, Horney believes that infant's helplessness leads not so much to focused sense of interiority, with competing drive to become superior. Rather infant's helplessness generates a *need for security*. This is the need that is significant in all neurosis. The expediency with which the neurotics try to cope with a world brings problem. Horney terms it *safety devices*. Thus, Adler's neurotic derive to power is interpreted by Horney as the need to pile up personal insurance against the danger of being overwhelmed. Mankind is and should be assertive. Assertion beyond the normal range is a means of coping with insecurity. The longing for love is fine; yet longing for unlimited support is another faulty means of coping with insecurity.

Hostility plays a basic role in Horney's thinking. However, she repudiates Freud's instinctual concept of hostility and aggression. According to her, the realistic frustration of normal desires awakens feelings of hostility. Furthermore, self-imposed neurotic frustrations also generate hostility.

Self-concept is another concept that looms large. The need to value oneself and to be valued is one of the finest attributes in man. Normally the person has an ideal for himself which serves as a guiding force in his behaviour. Only in neurosis does an idealized image of the self becomes too limited.

Conflict is another concept that bulks large in Horney's dynamics. Horney contends that both internal and external factors in man's experience foster the development of conflict. Driven by the need for integration, the neurotic is prone to solve the conflict by *repressing* one side of it. Repression does not eliminate. On this point, Horney agrees with Freud.

Horney's concept of the normal – actually the ideal – personality is not explicitly and systematically stated but appears as the rich, multiform obverse of the neurotic trends which she describes acutely.

Terms of the Milliea
The infantile experiences are never wholly without importance, but they are viewed as really "determining" only for the more inflexible and deeply neurotic patients.

The basic evil in home is the lack of warmth and affection, almost always a consequence of the neuroticism of parents. The child can accept realistic hardship provided that he feels essentially loved, accepted, appreciated. In the neurotic home, the child experiences unrealistic expectation.

Functioning of Personality

Horney's dynamics are similar to Adler's (attempt to envisage human behaviour as a constant effort at adaptation). However, Horney manes makes more use than Adler of the concept of the unconscious as a significant factor in itself. Aspects of the personality are genuinely repressed – almost in the Freudian sense of the term _ because they awaken intolerable anxiety.

Another important concept advanced by Horney involves the *idealized image of oneself*. Horney presents the tension between the idealized self and real self as major source of conflict, so major source of neurosis.

Feminine Psychology. A significant contribution of Horney involves her approach to feminine psychology. Horney was never a student of Freud, but did study his work and eventually taught psychoanalysis at both the Berlin and New York Psychoanalytic Institute. In many ways, Horney was ahead of her time. Although she died before the feminist movement took hold, she changed the way psychology looked at gender differences. She countered Freud's concept of *penis envy* with what she called womb envy, or men's envy of women's ability to bear children. She argued that men compensate for this inability by striving for achievement and success in other domains. She also disagreed with Freud's belief that males and females were born with inherent differences in their personality. According to Horney the differences were product of societal and cultural conditioning.

Neurosis. Horney's contribution towards understanding of neurosis is remarkable. She defined neurosis as a maladaptive and counterproductive way of dealing with relationships. These people are unhappy and desperately seek out relationship in order to feel good about themselves.

She identified three ways of dealing with the world: Moving toward people, moving against people, and moving away from people. Some children who feel a great deal of anxiety and helplessness *move toward people* in order to seek help and acceptance. They strive to feel worthy and can believe the only way to gain this is through the acceptance of others. These people have an intense need to be liked and appreciated. Their attempt to make that person love them creates a clinginess and neediness that may result in the other person leaving the relationship.

Another way (move against people) to deal with insecurities and anxieties is to try to force your power onto others in hopes of feeling good about yourself. Those with this personality style come across as bossy, demanding, selfish and even cruel. Horney argued that these people project their own hostilities with others.

The final possible consequence (move away from people) of a neurotic personality style is filled with asocial behaviour and an almost indifference to others. While it protects them from emotional pain of relationship, it also keeps away all positive aspects of relationships. It leaves them alone and empty.

Contribution

Karen Horney made significant contributions to

humanism, self-psychology, psychoanalysis and feminine psychology. Her refutation of Freud's theories about women generated much interest in the psychology of women. Horney also believed that people were able to act as their own therapists, emphasizing the personal role each person has in their own mental health and encouraging self-analysis and self-help.

Erich Fromm

Erich Fromm was born in Germany in 1900. He grew up a Jew in a country full of anti-Semitism. He witnessed World War I when he was an early teen and the rise of the Nazi party fifteen years later. His interest in war and politics grew from these experiences and much of his theories were derived as a result of his desire to understand why individual follow leaders into acts of destruction.

His initial book, and likely his most influential work was called Escape From Freedom, published near the beginning of World War II. In it he described freedom as the greatest problem for most individuals. With freedom according to Fromm, comes an overwhelming sense of alienation and an inability to exert individual power. He argued that we use several different techniques to reduce the anxiety associated with out perception of freedom. These techniques include automation / conformity, authoritarianism, destructiveness, and individuation.

The most common of these is **automation / conformity**. Fromm argued that with the anxiety associated with our inability to express power and our fear of aloneness, we conform ourselves to a larger society. By acting like everyone else, holding same values, purchasing the same products, and believing in the same morals, we gain a sense of power. The power of the masses assists us in not feeling alone and helpless. Unfortunately, according to Fromm, it also removes our individuality and prevents us from truly being ourselves.

Authoritarianism is a technique that others use to ward off the anxiety. As the individuals feel alone and powerless, they gain strength from the belief that there is a greater power beyond themselves. The entity could be a religious figure, a political leader or social belief. By giving up power to the powerful, we become powerful and no longer feel alone.

Others use the techniques Fromm called **destructiveness**, which refers to an attempt to destroy those we perceive as having the power. Because of our desire for power, we may feel that this finite resource must be taken from those who possess it. There are many ways to attempt this destruction, including the alignment with hate groups, religious extremism or even patriotism. While our actions are often antisocial, cruel, and misguided, we rationalize them by claiming a sense of duty, a god given order, or the love of country.

Fromm believed that all three of these techniques used to overcome our anxiety associated with freedom are unhealthy. The only healthy techniques is to embrace the freedom and express our true selves rather than what we perceive as giving us power. He argued that true power comes from individuality and freedom and doing what you went to do rather than what you are supposed to do is the only way to achieve **individuation**, the ability to be yourself.

Erich Fromm's major background is sociology rather than medicine. His most original contribution has been towards psychoanalytic approach to social problems. His social orientation is deeply related to his concept of individual.

Fromm seems less antagonistic to the Freudian libido theory than do Adler and Horney. Bodily (sexual) needs are frankly acknowledged as universal. Yet individual differences in temperament are given explicit importance. Fromm contends "specifically human problems begin where these matters leave off".

Fromm's imagination is caught by the panorama of biological evolution. The point he stresses is the growing *individuation* of the organism, reaching its culmination in man. Beyond all the creatures, man has freed himself from the matrix of nature is least bound either by outside events or by his so called instincts. He can create his own destiny.

Individuation is not an easy process. The little of Fromm's first book, *Escape from Freedom*, presents his position vividly. According to Fromm, persons experience conflict between the biologically conditioned instincts and the socially administered authoritarian commands (promising security). But human resources at disposal may pave the way for creative solution of the conflict. In *Man for Himself*, Fromm emphasizes the human potential.

Self-interest is a key element in process of individuation. There is no intrinsic contradiction between self-love and altruism (love and consideration for fellow-beings). According to Fromm, only the persons who love themselves are capable of appreciating the selfhood of others. Only such persons can love others generously.

As pointed out early Horney believes that individual is normally secure unless the conditions of life have fostered neurotic trends. Fromm suggests that a measure of uneasiness is universal and normally the person has some means of escaping it. Neurosis then becomes a matter of degree to which the individual is unable to literate the status as a separate self and has developed non productive mechanisms of escape.

There are existential problems of the human situation. Fromm does not blink them. Fromm writes: "Uncertainty is the very condition to impel man to unfold his powers. If he faces the truth without panic he will recognize that *there is no meaning to life* except the *meaning man gives his life by the unfolding of his powers.*

However, apart from the existential problems, there are historical problems such as war and poverty. Hence the data of psychology should be used in conjunction with materials from the natural and social sciences. Only humanistic ethics, rooted in the powers of man and the potential of his understanding can create a good society. It rests with man's courage to be himself and to be for himself.

Terms of the Milliea

Fromm focuses upon the tension between the impulse towards individuation and the security of primary emotional ties experience by the infant.

Fromm also considers the "marketing" orientation characteristic for modern capitalistic economics.

Functioning of Personality

Fromm, like Adler & Horney, emphasizes climate of the home, the need of the young child ofr warmth, affection and respect. Fromm is less repecting of the Freudian contribution towards analysis of the specific biological orientation of the child more emphasis on self-love.

Fromm's contribution is one of emphasizing the self.

Harry Stack – Sullivan

Sullivan presents *interpersonal relations* the whole

story of human psychology. Sullivan had his training in the William Alanson White Psychiatric Foundation. This school sponsored an excellent journal, *Psychiatry*. Sullivan is the least reductionist. For him, *modes of interaction* is the real focus of psychological inquiry. Sullivan defines all situations in interpersonal terms. Even our most solitary experiences are related to "fantasized person fixations" developed in the course of our experience with people.

Sullivan main theoretical concern seems to be with the *complete integration of organism and milieu*. Sullivan goes on to point out that maintenance of life *requires* interchange with environment. The human infont is poorly equipped for such interchanges at birth, although well equipped for ultimate highly adaptive interchange. As growth and maturation proceed acculturation is inevitable.

The point Sullivan stresses again and again is the functional unity of the self developing in its interpersonal context. Very often the contours of the *situation* as viewed from outside seem to have very little to do with the psychological reaction of the person. Some people surmount easily situations that seem to us crashing or they may collapse at what seems to us a quite a trivial. This judgment is true even when our evaluation of the situation is not very personally our own but has what Sullivan calls *consensual validation* (the evaluation is what most of us would agree upon).

Sullivan makes use of the concept of *self dynamism*. Self dynamism is a relatively permanent configuration of energy which manifests in interpersonal relation. The self-dynamism comes to play a crucial role in the organization of behaviour. It is built out of child's experience. It is made of reflected appraisals. It comes into being as a dynamism to preserve the feeling of security. It is build largely of elements learned in contact with other significant people.

Initially the organism pursues satisfaction implicit in its bodily structure. The end state desired is called euphoria, a condition of tensionless bliss most nearly approximated by dreamless sleep. Later the *pursuit of security* arises. This pursuit is culturally determined and comes to involve the need for approval and prestige. The enduring configuration develops out of the reflected appraisals of the significant adults around the infant and becomes a factor of prime dynamic importance for all human behaviour. For Sullivan, as for the other psychoanalysts the major contours of the self are established rather enduringly in the very early years of childhood and provide the main orientation of the personality towards later experience.

As pointed out earlier, Sullivan was trained in psychoanalysis in the United States, but soon drifted from the specific psychoanalytic belief while retaining much of the core concepts of Freud. Interestingly Sullivan placed a lot of focus on both the social aspects of personality and cognitive representations. This moved him away from Freud's psychosexual development and toward a more eclectic approach.

Freud believed that anxiety was an important aspect in his theory because it represented internal conflict between the id and the superego. Sullivan, however saw anxiety as existing only as a result of social interaction. He described techniques, much like defense mechanisms, that provide tools for people to use in order to reduce social anxiety. **Selective inattention** is one such mechanism.

According to Sullivan, mothers show their anxiety about child rearing to their children through various means. The child, having no way to deal with this, feels the anxiety himself. Selective inattention is soon learned, and the child begins to ignore or reject the anxiety or any interaction that could produce these uncomfortable feelings. As adults we use the technique to focus our minds **away** from stressful **situations**.

Personifications

Through social interaction and our selective attention or inattention, we develop what Sullivan calls **personifications** of ourselves and others. While defenses can often help reduce anxiety, they can also lead to a misperception of reality. Again Sullivan shifts his attention from Freud and move toward a cognitive approach to understanding personality.

These personifications are mental images that allow us to better understand ourselves and the world. There are three basic ways we see ourselves that Sullivan called the **bad-me**, the **good-me** and the **not-me**. The bad-me represents those aspects of the self that are considered negative and are therefore hidden from others and possibly even the self. The anxiety we feel is often a result of recognition of the bad part of ourselves, such as when we recall an embarrassing moment or experience guilt from a past action.

The good-me is everything we like about ourselves; It represents the part of us we share with others and that we often choose to focus on because it produces no anxiety. The final part of is, called the not-me, represents all those things that are so anxiety-provoking that we can not even consider them a part of us. Doing so would definitely create anxiety which we spend our lives trying to avoid. The not-me is kept out of awareness by pushing it deep into the unconscious.

Developmental Epochs

Another similarity between Sullivan's theory and that of Freud's is the belief that childhood experiences determine, to a larger degree, the adult personality. And, throughout our childhood the mother plays the most significant role. Unlike Freud, however, he believed that personality can develop past adolescence and even well into adulthood. He called the stages in his developmental **Epochs**. He believed that we pass through these stages in a particular order but the timing of such is dictated by our social environment. Much of the focus in Sullivan's theory revolved around the concept of adolescence. As can be seen from the Exhibit three stages are devoted to the period of adolescence.

Exhibit

Developmental Epochs	Age Norms	Characteristics
Infancy	Birth to 1 year	The child begins the process of development. Yet it does not carry the same importance as indicated by Freud
Childhood	1 to 5 years	The development of speech and improved communication
Juvenile	5 to 8 years	Focus is on the need for the playmates. Beginning of health socialization
Preadolescence	9 to 12 years	Ability to form a close relationship with a peer. This relationship will later assist in feeling worthy and likable
Early adolescence	13 to 17 years	The onset of puberty. Self-work becomes synonymous with sexual attractiveness and acceptance by the opposite sex
Late Adolescence	18 to 22/23 years	Need for friendship or sexual expression. Conflict between parental control and self-expression are visible
Adulthood	Age 23 on	The struggles of adulthood include financial security, career and family

Functioning of Personality

Based on his model of interpersonal relation, Sullivan conceptualized a taxonomy of personality. The taxonomy can be presented as follows.

Exhibit 2

Functioning Type	Special Feature
1. Non integrative person	Psychopathic
2. Self-absorbed	Wishful Thinking
3. Incorrigible	
4. Negativistic	Hostile, unfriendly
5. Stammerer	
6. Ambition-ridden	
7. Asocial	
8. Inadequate	
9. Homosexual	
10. Chronically adolescent	Too much dependency
	(Always pursues idea, buy never finds it)

Conclusion

Sullivan was trained in American psychiatry, with William Alonson White and Adolf Meyer rather than with Freud as his early mentor. He remained much more closely involved with hospital work than with psychoanalysis. Schizophrence was a sort of specialty for him. He developed an extensive consultation practice and was deeply concerned with teaching and with the selection of young candidates for training in psychiatry.

Otto Rank

Otto Rank was a member of Freud's early coterie and

a powerful figure in the young psychoanalytic movement. He was not a doctor of medicine. His background and training were in the areas of engineering, philosophy, psychology and art. In the early 100's, Freud welcomed the difference Freud almost assigned the expansion of analytic theory in the area of "culture" to this brilliant young outsider. Sympathetic relations prevailed for more than twenty years, but gradually became strained to the breaking point. Rank preferred to call his technique *psychotherapy* rather than psychoanalysis.

Rank's major impact has been through the field of social work – the "functional" approach. In the late 1920's, he undertook the professional task of helping troubled families to better social functioning. He also lectured at the important schools of social work in the USA.

The Birth Trauma

Among the various biological emphases of Freud's early theories, it was the *trauma of birth* which caught Rank's attention. In 1926, Freud ascribed this event as the prototype of anxiety.

Rank felt that the change from the all-encompassing, effortless bliss of the womb to the painful hurlyburly of postnatal conditions requiring initiative from the infant was actually determining for life. The most normal among us carry a load of *primary anxiety*. The human goal is reinstatement of embryonic bliss and the greatest human error is *separation*. The overwhelming trauma of the births experience is repressed (*Primary repression*). The central human conflict thus becomes the wash to return to the womb versus terrible fear associated with birth.

Many symbolism (such as man's caves, sitting

postures during depression) were interpreted in terms of wish to return to womb.

Genitality was interpreted for the male as a re=entrance into the mother's body – the only possible return to the womb. The female is denied such direct return. Yet her love relationship is indirectly explained.

Concentration on the birth-trauma led Rank more and more towards an emphasis on the powerful movements of the personality as a whole. Although Rank and Adler and Jung are different in many respects, they have in common an insistence on the primary of the personality as a whole, the self.

The Will

The name Rank gives to the integrative power of the personality as a whole is the *will*. It is the consequence of being born and of living, a *necessary* development of the human organism.

Rank assigns to the will a central position in his theory of personality and therapy. Man is not merely the battle-ground of impulses at war with one another and with external pressures. The very core of his being is his *active* relationship to himself and his world – hi "will".

Therapy must address itself primarily to this active will. Its main instrument is the relationship between the patient and therapist. The essential task of therapy is not to give the patient insight, or even an re-education. Therapy succeeds only in so far as the will orientation of the patient is changed.

Later Position

(1)   In order to define his own self, the person defines himself to himself. This brings conflict with parents and others.

In the therapeutic relation; self acceptance becomes possible through the "love experiences" of being accepted by other person.

Imp – self acceptance as a key concern.

(2)   Less emphasis on the physiological event of passage through the birth canal and more emphasis on an essentially philosophical antithesis between separation and uncon, of life and death.

The essential point is the polarity between life and death, between separation (individuation à life-fear) and union (loss of individuality à death-fear). The necessary human conflict, according to rank, leads to three concepts. (1) Fear becomes a constructive force rather than crippling anxiety. (2) Resistance, at least potentially the constructive power of the will. (3) The major ideal of human race is to attain constructive, creative intepration of the trends towards uncon and separation.

Rank's term for the person who achieves this pattern of creative reintegration is the *artist*. Those who fail to achieve this are *average man* and *the neurotic*.

The neurotic and the artist have the fundamental point in common. They have committed themselves to the points of separation, from the herd (from unreflected incorporation of the views of their society). But the artist is essentially able to achieve integration of his separate will and his need for union through a creative relationship to "others".

The neurotic does not win through to this constructive bringing together of the basic dichotomous trends. The neurotic has achieved or been forced onto a sense of his separateness so great that, the adjustment is adversely affected.

Average man represents the first and easiest solution of the problem set by birth – This essentially adoption undivided has a relatively harmonious relationship to his society, but only because he has never truly differentiated his own will from the significant surroundings. Rank does not lies average man. He concerns himself with an individual: the neurotics and the artist.

Chapter : 6

Behavioural Counselling

Several names emerge as contributors to behavioural counseling, including Pavlov, Watson, Thorndike and Wolpe. However, the name that best known to the general public is B.F. Skinner. Skinner's methods are widely known today by psychotherapists, educators, counselors, and parents.

Skinner's contribution to knowledge is not strictly confined to the laboratory. He made considerable contributions to solving educational problems. Perhaps the most significant of Skinner's contribution is *Beyond Freedom and Dignity*, in which he pictures a society where behaviour is shaped and controlled by a planned system of rewards. Summing up his 62 years in the profession, Skinner (1990) said that the point he tried to make is that it can be demonstrated that people choose behaviour based on anticipated consequences.

The Nature of People

Behaviourists view human beings as neither good nor bad but merely as products of their environment. People are essentially born neutral (the blank slate, or *tabula rasa*), with equal potential for good or evil and for rationality or irrationality.

Behaviourists view people as responders. They reject self-directing mentalistic concepts of human behaviour.

Behaviourists contend that people can make only those responses they have learned, and they make them when the stimulus conditions are appropriate.

Individuals are viewed by behavioural counselors as products of their conditioning. The stimulus response paradigm is the basic pattern of all human learning. People react in predictable ways to any given stimulus according to what they have learned through experience. Humans react to stimuli in much the same way animals do, except that human responses are more complex and are organized on a higher plane.

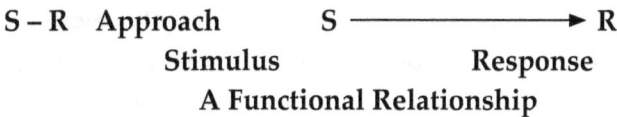

S – R   Approach   S ——————————► R
           Stimulus   **Response**
        A Functional Relationship

Skinner regarded the human being as an organiser who learns patterns of behaviours. To be more specific, the organism learns a specific response when a satisfying condition (**reinforcement**) follows an action. The number of these responses mounts as time passes and satisfying conditions are repeated. The following *principles of reinforcement* are important:

1. Behaviour followed by satisfying state of affairs is strengthened.

2. Behaviour followed by the withdrawal of reinforcement or dissatisfying state of   affairs is weakened and ultimately eliminated.

Since human behaviour is learned, any or all behaviour can be unlearned and new behaviours learned in its place. This is the most fundamental principle of

behavioural counselling. The behaviourist is concerned with observable events. These observable events, when they become unacceptable behaviours, can be unlearned. It is this unlearning or reeducation process with which the behavioural counselor is concerned.

The Principle

Behavioural counseling is a reeducation, or relearning, process. Adaptive or helpful behaviour is reinforced, while maladaptive or unhelpful behaviour is extinguished. The counsellor's role is, through reinforcement principles to help clients achieve the goals they have set for themselves.

Behavioural counseling includes several techniques based on the principles of learning employed to manage maladaptive behaviour. Today, behavioural counseling is used with covert processes (cognitions, emotions, obsessive ideation) as well as traditional, overt behaviour problems. Behavioural counseling involves two types of behaviour : operant and respondent

	Present	Remove
Positive stimuli (incentive, praise, free time)	Positive reinforcement	Extinction
Negative stimuli (blaming, criticism, loss of free time)	Punishment	Negative reinforcement

Examples of operant conditioning

In operant conditioning, *operant behaviour* refers to behaviour that operates on and changes the environment in some manner. It is also referred to as "instrumental behaviour" because it is instrumental in goal achievement. People who use operant conditioning wait until the desired behaviour or an approximation of the desired behaviour occurs and then reinforce it with a rewarding stimulus known as *positive reinforcement* (praise, money, free time, and the like). *Negative reinforcement* (different from punishment) occurs when the operant behaviour is reinforced by its capacity to stop an aversive stimulus. For example, rats well learn to press a bar to shut off an electric shock, and employees will go to their work desks to shut off the aversive sound of their manager's scolding. *Punishment,* like positive reinforcement occurs after the behaviour is emitted but tends to decrease its occurrence. *Extinction* is the process of eliminating a learned behaviour by ignoring the behaviour or by not reinforcing it through attention and other rewards (withdrawal of rewards is privileges). Figure may help explain these options.

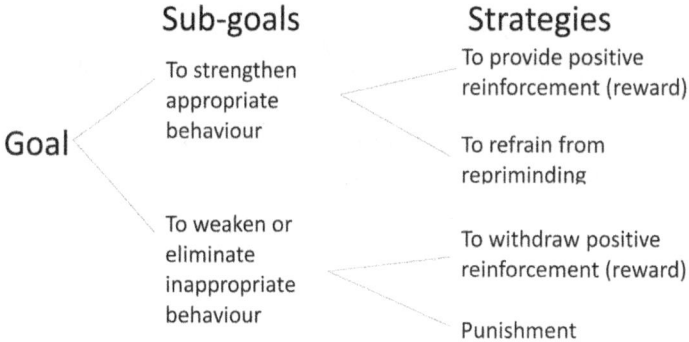

	Sub-goals	Strategies
	To strengthen appropriate behaviour	To provide positive reinforcement (reward)
Goal		To refrain from repriminding
	To weaken or eliminate inappropriate behaviour	To withdraw positive reinforcement (reward)
		Punishment

Counseling Methods

The goal of a behavioural counselor can be organized into three main categories

1.   Altering maladaptive behaviour;
2.   Teaching the decision-making process; and
3.   Preventing problems.

A number of counseling techniques are available.

Behaviour Analysis

It is important to note that behaviour consists of three phases :

- **antecedent**, the stimulus or cue that occurs before behaviour that leads to its occurrence;
- **behaviour**, what the person says or does (or doesn't); and
- **consequence**, what the person perceives happens to himself or herself (positive, negative, and neutral) as a result of his or her behaviour

Behaviour problems are usually rooted in antecedents or consequences.

Operant Techniques

A number of operant techniques can be adopted.

Contingency contracting. The use of this technique can be broken down into six steps:

1. The counsellor and the employee identify the problem to be solved
2. Data are collected to verify the baseline frequency rate for the occurrence of the undesired behaviour
3. The counselor and the employee set mutually acceptable goals
4. Specific counseling techniques are selected for attaining the goals
5. The counseling techniques are evaluated for

observable and measurable change
6. Step 4 is repeated if the selected techniques are not effective. If the techniques prove effective, a maintenance plan is developed for maintaining the new behaviour change.

Self-management. An adaptation of the six-step method, the self-management plan is designed for employees who are able to take more responsibility for their behaviours. These plans also follow a step-by-step process: defining a problem in behavioural terms, collecting data on the problem, introducing a remediation programme based on behaviour principles, evaluating the effectiveness, and appropriately changing the technique if the plan is not working. The major difference between self-management and other techniques is that employees assume major responsibility.

Shaping. The basic operant technique of shaping is a general procedure designed to induce new behaviours by reinforcing behaviours that approximate the desired behaviour. Each successive approximation of the behaviour is reinforced until the desired behaviour is obtained. To administer the technique, the counselor must know how to skillfully use (1) looking, (2) waiting, and (3) reinforcing. The counselor looks for the desired behaviour, waits until it occurs, and reinforces it when it does occur. In essence, the counselor is catching the employee in good behaviour – a much more difficult task than catching the employee in bad behaviour.

Modeling. Modeling consists of exposing the employee to one or more individual, either in real life or in film or tape presentation who exhibit behaviour to be adopted. Counselors may be the models to demonstrate certain behaviours to the employee, or peers of the employee may be used.

Peers and colleagues are an important part of the employee's world, and their influence could be used quite effectively to help employees change. People usually imitate the behaviours of persons they like. A model may be presented to the employee through the use of TV, films, videotapes, or books.

Token economies. Token economies are used on a group basis. The employees earn tokens or points for certain target behaviours. These behaviours are classified as being either on task or socially appropriate. Tokens or points also may be lost for off-task and socially inappropriate behaviours. Employees may periodically cash in tokens or points earned for such rewards as free time, game time, money, and the like.

Behaviour practice group. Behaviour practice group have some advantage. Members of group meet weekly and take up some helpful programmes such as communication skills or weight loss. The counselor supervises the progress objectively.

Classical Technique

Respondent behaviour is associated with classical conditioning, in which learning occurs when a stimulus that already elicits a response (an unconditioned stimulus is presented with a neutral stimulus that elicits no response or a different response. With repeated pairings of the two stimuli, the neutral stimulus begins to elicit the same response as does the unconditioned stimulus. In the case of Pavlov's dogs, for example, the unconditioned stimulus of food was paired with the neutral stimulus of a bell. The unconditioned stimulus was salivating. The neutral stimulus (the bell) became the conditioned stimulus, and the response to the conditioned stimulus became the conditioned response (salivating).

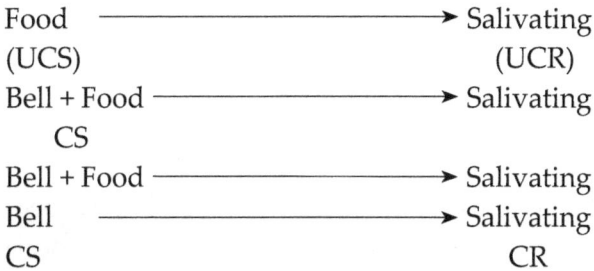

Food ⟶ Salivating
(UCS) (UCR)
Bell + Food ⟶ Salivating
CS
Bell + Food ⟶ Salivating
Bell ⟶ Salivating
CS CR

Counter-conditioning. In counter-conditioning, a stronger pleasant stimulus is paired with a weaker aversive stimulus as a procedure for overcoming the anxiety the aversive stimulus evokes. For example, an individual may be given his or her favorite gift while a sitting in the inhospitable room. If the gift is sufficiently rewarding to the individual, the anxiety evoked by the room would be diminished.

Systematic desensitization. It was developed by Wolpe. It is based on the principle of counter-conditioning. An employee may be experiencing anxiety related to specific stimulus such as performing in front of a group. The first step is to develop a hierarchy of scenes related to the fear, with mildly aversive scenes at the bottom and progressively more aversive scenes at the top. The individual is then taught the deep relaxation process and, while relaxed, is asked to visualize the various scenes in the hierarchy.

Chapter : 7

Cognitive Restructuring

In behavioural counselling, the emphasis has been on the direct manipulation of overt behaviour and occasionally of covert behaviour. Relatively little attention has been paid to direct alteration of the thinking and reasoning process of the client. Perhaps behaviour counsellors initially discounted the importance of cognition, regarding any appeal to thinking as a return to the "mentalism". However, recently behaviour counsellors have paid attention to "private events" – to thoughts, perceptions, judgments, and self-statements – and they have studied and manipulated these processes in their attempts to understand and modify overt and covert disturbed behaviour.

Cognitive restructuring is a general term for changing pattern of thought that is presumed to be causing a disturbed emotion. It is carried out in several ways by cognitive behaviour counsellors. The contribution of two eminent psychologists, Ellis and Beck, are important in this context.

Ellis's Rational-Emotive Counselling

The principal thesis of Ellis's rational emotive (REC) counselling is that sustained emotional reactions are caused by internal sentences that people repeat to themselves. The aim of counselling is to eliminate the wrongheaded beliefs of disturbed people through a rational examination of them.

Nature of People

It is believed that "what disturb men's minds is not events, but their judgment of events." REC does not concentrate upon the past events in one's life, but rather on present events and how one reacts to them. REC stresses that, as human beings, we have choices. We control our ideas, altitudes, feelings, and actions, and we arrange our lives according to own our dictates. We have little control over what happens or what actually exists, but we do have both choices and control over how we view the world, and how we react to difficulties, regardless of how we have been taught to respond.

REC theory holds that people are neither good nor bad, if they respond to others with a rational belief system. If people react with irrational beliefs, however, they will view themselves and others as evil and horrible whenever they or others fall short of expectations. Ellis (1987) views humans as naturally irrational, self-defeating individuals who need to be taught otherwise. They think crookedly about their desires and preferences and escalate them self-defeatingly into musts, should, oughts and demands. In assimilating these irrational beliefs, people become emotionally disturbed and feel anger, anxiety, depression, worthlessness, self-pity and other negative feelings that lead to destructive behaviour. However, Ellis has also stated that people can be "naturally" helpful and loving *as long as they do not think irrationally*. In other words, Ellis has described a circular process, as depicted in the following figure.

Irrational thinking leads to self-hate, which leads

to self-destructive behaviour and eventually to hatred of others, which in turn causes others to act irrationally towards the individual and thus to begin the cycle again.

The Principle

Ellis theorized that individuals' responses or belief towards the same events are predicted upon their belief systems.

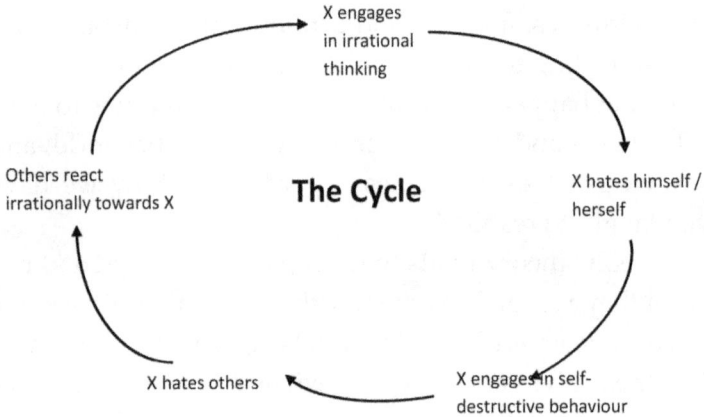

These individual belief systems are what people tell themselves about an event – in particular, an unfortunate incident.

People hold tenaciously to their beliefs, rational or not. Consequently, the counsellor vigorously attacks the irrational beliefs in an attempt to show employees how illogical they think. Using the Socratic method of questioning and disputing, the counsellor takes a verbally active part in the early stages of counselling by identifying and explaining the employees' problems. If counsellor guesses correctly, which often happens, they

argue with and persuade the employee to give up the erratic view and replace with a new, essentially useful orientation.

Ellis suggests that, to the usual psychotherapeutic techniques of exploration, ventilation and interruptions, the rational counsellor adds techniques of confrontation, indoctrination and reeducation.

Counselling Process

To achieve the aims, the counsellor has specific tasks. The first step is to show clients that they have incorporated many irrational "should", "oughts", and "musts". Clients learn to separate their irrational beliefs from their rational ones.

A second step in the counselling process takes clients beyond the stage of awareness. It demonstrates that they keep their emotional disturbances active by continuing to think illogically and by repeating self-defeating meanings and philosophies. To get beyond client's mere recognition of irrational thoughts and feelings the counsellor takes a third step, helping them modify their thinking and abandon their irrational idea.

The fourth and final step in the counselling process is to challenge, clients to develop a rational philosophy of life so that in the future they can avoid becoming the victim of other irrational beliefs.

Techniques

Counsellors use a number of techniques. Some of the evocative techniques include the following:

Rational-emotive imagery. Clients imaging themselves thinking, feeling and behaving exactly the way they would like think, feel and behave in real life. They can also be shown how to imagine one of the worst thinking that could happen to them, how to feel inappropriately upset about the situation, how to intensely experience their feeling and then how to change the experience to an appropriate feeling.

Role playing. There are both emotional and behavioural components in role playing. The counsellor often interrupts to show clients what they are telling themselves to create disturbances and what they can do to change their inappropriate feelings to appropriate ones.

Shame-attacking exercise. These are exercises which help people get rid of irrational shame over behaving in certain ways. He thinks that we can stubbornly refuse to feel ashamed by telling ourselves that it is not catastrophic if someone thinks we are foolish. The main point of these exercises is that clients work to feel unashamed even when others clearly disapprove of them.

Use of force and vigour. The use of force and energy help the clients to go from intellectual to emotional insight. Clients are also shown how to conduct forceful dialogues with themselves in which they express their irrational beliefs and then powerfully dispute them.

Human nature has the potential to be both rational (scientific approach) and irrational (departure from science). The REC concept of self-acceptance means that a person is more than a set of behaviours. That is, people are better off negating specific behaviours without labeling their entire self as good or bad.

Beck's cognitive counselling makes use of persuasive communication instead of Ellis's confrontation. How can the counselling help the individual to alter his or her dysfunctional assumptions? In addition to verbal persuasion, the counsellor may encourage the clients to behave in ways inconsistent with them. For example, a woman who believes that she must please everyone at her office can decline the next unreasonable request made of her and see whether, as she has been assuming, the sky will fall. If the situation has been analyzed ahead of time by client and counsellor, clearly a necessary step, the woman can experience what happens when she acts against her absolutist belief.

The views and techniques of Ellis and Beck are widely used by counsellors these days. However, inventive counsellors make some changes as they apply to specific clients.

Chapter : 8

Cognitive Behaviour Therapy

In today's world, cognitive behaviour therapy (CBT) is the most preferred mode of therapy. It blends the best elements of behaviour therapy and cognitive therapy. The traditional behaviour therapy moved in the direction of cognitive behaviour therapy. Several of the move prominent cognitive behavioural approach include Albert Ellis's rational emotive behaviour therapy (REBT), Aaron Beck's and Judith Beck's cognitive therapy and Donald Meichenbaum's cognitive behaviour therapy (CBT). The CBT combines both cognitive and behavioural principles and methods; it has generated more empirical research than any other psychotherapy model.

Although proponents slightly vary in their approaches, they do share some common features. (1) a collaborative relationship between client and therapist, (2) a premise that psychological distress is largely a function of disturbances in cognitive processes, (3) a focus on changing cognitions to produce desired changes in affect and behaviour, (4) a present-centered, time-limited focus, (5) an active and direct stance by the therapist, and (6) a focus on targeted problem.

Both the cognitive therapy and cognitive behaviour therapy are based on the assumption that a reorganization of one's self-statements will result in a corresponding reorganization of one's behaviour.

Albert Ellis's **Rational Emotive Behaviour Therapy (REBT)** is the first of the cognitive behaviour therapy. It stresses thinking, judging, deciding, analyzing and doing. The basic assumption of REBT is that people contribute to their own psychological problems and to specific programs by the rigid and extreme beliefs they have about events and situations. REBT posits that cognitions emotions and behaviours interact significantly and have a reciprocal cause-and-effect relationship.

Ellis gave credit to Alfred Adler as an influential precursor of REBT, and Karen Horney's idea on the "tyranny of the should". REBT's basic hypothesis is that our emotions stem mainly from our beliefs, which influence the evaluations and interpretations we make of the reactions we have to life situations. Through therapy clients learn skills that give the tools to identify and dispute irrational beliefs that have been acquiring and self-constructed and are now maintained by self-indoctrination.

The A-B-C framework is control to REBT therapy and practice

A (activating event) → B (Belief) → C (Emotional and Behavioural Consequences)

D (Disputing intervention) → E (Effect) → F (New Feeling)

The framework is self-explanatory.

Aaron Beck and his daughter Judith Beck pioneered cognitive therapy. Aaron Beck developed and validated Beck's Depression Inventory (BDI) which is the most frequently used test (only next to intelligence test) in the world. She and her father founded Back Institute for Cognitive Therapy in Philadelphia. The essential featured of Beck's cognitive therapy hs been described in the previous chapter.

Donald Meichenbaum

Donald Meichenbaum was born in New Yok City and started his career at the University of Waterloo, Canada. He conducted research on the development of cognitive behaviour therapy (CBT). He received recognition for his work on suicide prevention.

Meichenbaum attributed the origin of CBT to his mother who had a knack for telling stories about her daily activities that were peppered with her thoughts, feeling, and running commentaries. This childhood experience contributed to Meichenbaum's psychotherapeutic approach. He encouraged his clients to tell their stories and describe what they did to "survive and cope".

According to Meichenbaum, self-statement affects a person's behaviour in much the same way as statements made by other person. A basic premise of CBT is that clients must notice how they think, feel and behave. For change to occur clients need to interrupt the scripted nature of their behaviour so that they can evaluate their behaviour in various situations.

Changing Clients' Self-Verbalizations

Meichenbaum (1977) proposes that behaviour change occur through a sequence of mediating processes involving the interaction of inner speech, cognitive structures, and behaviours and their resultant outcomes. It includes several phases of change.

Phase 1: Self-Observation. The beginning step in the change process consists of clients' learning how to observe their own behaviour. When clients begin therapy, their interous dialogue is characterized by negative self-statements and imagery. A critical factor is their willingness and ability to listen to themselves.

This process involve an increased sensitivity to their thoughts, feeling, actions, physiological fraction and ways of reacting to others. If depressed clients hope to make positive changes, they are not victims of negative thoughts and feelings. Rather, they are actually contributing to their depression through the thing they tell themselves.

Phase 2: Starting a new interna dialogue. As a result of early client-counsellor contact, clients learn to notice their maladaptive behaviours. They begin to see opportunities of adaptive behaviours themselves. If clients hope to change they may tell themselves that they must initiate a new behavioural chain. They initiate positive internal verbalizations that serve as guide.

Phase 3: Learning new Skills. The third phase of modification process consists of helping clients interrupt the downward spiral of thinking, feeling and behaving. They learn more adaptive ways of coping. Clients focus on telling themselves new sentences and observing and assessing the outcomes.

Stress Inoculation Training

A special application of coping skills programme is teaching clients management techniques by way of a strategy known as stress inoculation training (SIT). The process involves the following sequence of activities:

- Expose clients to anxiety – provoking situation by means of role playing and imagery
- Require clients to evaluate their anxiety level
- Teach clients to become aware of the anxiety-provoking cognitions they experience in stressful situations
- Help clients examine these thoughts by reevaluating their self-statements

- Have clients note the level of anxiety following this reevaluation

An Evaluation of CBT

All of the cognitive behavioural approaches stress the importance of cognitive processes as determinants of behaviour. It is assumed that how people feel and what they actually do is largely influenced by their subjective assessment and interpretations of situations. Because this appraisal of life situations is influenced by beliefs, attitudes, assumptions and internal dialogues cognitions become major focus of therapy.

The cognitive behavioural approaches focus on undermining faulty assumptions and belief and teaching clients the coping skills needed to deal with their problems. Both Ellis's REBT and Beck's CT are based on a wide range of cognitive behavioural techniques and follow a defined plan of actions. They are relatively brief and structured treatments in keeping with the spirit of cost-effectiveness and evidence-based practice. The psychoeducational aspect of CBT is a clear strength that can be applied to many problems and used effectively in many setting with diverse client populations including organizational employees.

Chapter : 9

Humanistic and Existential Counselling

Humanistic and existential counselling, like psychoanalytic counselling, are insight – oriented. These are based on the assumption that disordered behaviours can best be treated by increasing the individual's awareness of motivations and needs. But there is a difference between psychoanalytic orientation and humanistic-existential perspective. The humanistic-existential approach places greater emphasis on the person's freedom of choice.

Nature of People

Free will is regarded as the human being's most important characteristic. Free will is, however, a double-edged sword, for it not only offers fulfillment and pleasure but also threatens acute pain and suffering. It is a gift that must be used and that requires special courage to use. Not all of us can meet this challenge; those who cannot are considered as candidates for counselling.

Carl Roger's Person-Centered Counselling

Rogers makes several basic assumptions about human nature and the means by which we can try to understand it.

1. We must adopt a phenomenological point of view. People can be understood only from the vantage point of their own perceptions and feelings. A person's phenomenological world is a major determinant of behaviour
2. Healthy people are aware of their behaviour
3. People are innately good and effective, they become ineffective and disturbed only when faulty learning intervenes.
4. Behaviour is purposive and goal-directed. They are self-directive.
5. Counsellors should not attempt to manipulate events for individual, rather they should create conditions that will facilitate independent decision making by the client.

Counselling Techniques

Assuming that a mature and well-adjusted person makes his or her own judgments based on what is intrinsically satisfying, Rogers avoids imposing goals on the client. The client is to take the lead and direct the course of conversation and of the session. The counsellor's job is to create conditions so that during their hour together the client can return once again to the basic nature and judge for himself or herself which course of life is intrinsically gratifying. Because of Roger's very positive view of people, he assumes that their decisions will not only make them happy with themselves but also turn them into good, civilized people.

Roger's thinking evolved from a clear specification of techniques to an emphasis on the attitude and emotional style of the counsellor and a de-emphasis of specific procedure. The counsellor should have three core qualities

Genuineness encompasses spontaneity, openness, and authenticity. The counsellor has no pretension in disclosing his/her professional facade. In a sense the counsellor through honest disclosure provides a model for what the client can become. The second attribute of the counsellor involves ability to extend **unconditional positive regard**. Rogers call it "condition of worth". The person-centered counsellor prizes clients as they are, and conveys unpossessive warmth for them, even if he/she does not approve of their behaviours.

The third quality, **accurate empathetic understanding,** is the ability to the world through the eyes of clients from moment to moment, to understand the feelings of clients both from their own phenomenological vantage point, which is known to them, and from perspectives that they may be only dimly aware of. Empathizing – the acceptance, recognition, and clarification of feelings – is one of the few techniques of Rogerian counselling. Within the context of a warm empathetic relationship, the counsellor encourages the client to talk about his or her most deeply felt concerns and attempts to restate the emotional aspects. Because feelings are mirrored back without judgment or disapproval, the client can look at them, clarify them, and acknowledge and accept them. Feared thoughts and emotions that were previously too threatening to enter awareness can become part of the self-concept.

The counsellor, it should be noted, is not being truly nondirective, a term applied to Rogers, for he selectively attends to evaluate statements and feelings expressed by the client.

If counselling conditions allowing self-acceptance are established, clients begin to talk in a more honest and emotional way about themselves. It is assumed that such talk in itself is primarily responsible for changing behaviour.

Counselling Procedure

The emphathetic relationship is the critical variable. In this framework, the main **techniques are listening, accepting, respecting, understanding, and sharing**. According to Combos, **the current person-centered approach is understood primarily as a process of helping clients discover new and more satisfying personal meaning for themselves and the world they inhabit.**

Applications

The approach is useful in the training of practitioners, because the methods have built-in safety features. For a person with limited background in counselling, personality dynamics and psychopathology, the approach offers the assurance that prospective clients will not be psychologically harmed. By extending the counselling conditions of genuineness, empathetic understanding, and unconditional positive regard to situations, many persons have been of assistance to help seekers.

Existential Counselling

The existential point of view, like humanism, emphasizes personal growth. The existential counselling grew because of the influence of the literary movement in existentialism. The Danish philosopher Kierkegaard and the German philosopher Husserl and Heidegger were the prominent thinkers. In addition, Austrian psychiatrist Viktor Frankl's views and logotherapy provided impetus for the growth of existential analysis.

Hamlet's famous soliloquy beginning "To be, or not

to be – that is the question" (Act III, Scene 1) is the classic existential statement. To be truly alive is to confront the anxiety that comes with existential choices. Existential anxiety comes from several sources. Second, we are aware that we must ultimately make decisions, act and live with the consequences. Third, we must ourselves create the meaning of our lives; the ultimate responsibility for endowing our world and our lives with substance and purpose rests with each of us. And finally, we know that we are ultimately alone.

The Goal of Counselling

A person is the sum of the choices he/she makes. Difficulties in making choices can be understood only by exploring experiences. The existential counsellor, by offering support and empathy through adopting of individual's phenomenological frame of reference, helps him/her explore his/her behaviour, feelings, relationship, and what his/her life means to him/her. But the counsellor also encourages the client to confront and clarify past and present choices. Present choices are the most important.

In addition, existential counsellor helps people relate *authentically* to others. People are asked to define their identity and existence in terms of their relationship.

The principal goal of existential counselling is to make the client more aware of his or her own potential for choice and growth. In the existential view people create their existence anew at each moment. The potential for disorder as well as for growth is ever present. Individuals must be encouraged to *accept their responsibility* for their own existence and to realize that, within certain limits, they can redefine themselves at any moment and feel differently within their own social environment. One of the goals of therapy is to bolster their resolve and ability to cope with this inescapable anxiety and to continue growing.

The existential experts, however, are very vague about what counselling techniques will help the client grow.

Chapter : 10

Counselling Sessions

Introduction

In the workplace, counselling is a discussion between a counsellor and an employee about an employee's performance. The discussion may focus on a specific incident, a particular aspect of an employee's performance which has been identified as in need of improvement, or in some instances, the employee's overall performance or behaviour. The goals of the discussion are:

- To communicate the counsellor's concerns to the employee
- To determine the cause of the employee's actions
- To identify avenues for improvement and/or development
- To improve the employee's performance.

Counselling is a positive and constructive supervisory tool. Because it involves face-to-face communication between the counsellor and the employee, it is the most direct and the most efficient means available to have a positive impact on the performance of an employee.

Unfortunately, the term "counselling" and "counselling memo" have become sensitive terms which stimulate strong reactions. One reason for this is that counselling is often mistaken for discipline.

Counselling is not discipline. The primary difference between counselling and discipline is that counselling attempts to correct performance issues through the use of face-to-face communication and problem solving, while discipline attempts to do so through the imposition of a penalty. For most types of performance and shortcoming, a supervisor should attempt to first deal with the issues through counselling. Disciplinary actions should be considered only when counselling fails.

Certainly, there are circumstances which require immediate disciplinary action. These include, but are not limited to, illegal, unethical, dishonest or highly inappropriate activities such as gross negligence, verbal or physical assault, accepting a bribe, insubordination, or theft or destruction of state-owned property. Supervisors confronted with such serious violations should immediately consult with their personnel and employee relations office.

The Sessions
Counsellors often avoid conducting counselling sessions with employees because the counsellors anticipate, sometimes correctly, that the session will be unpleasant. Most individuals simply do not enjoy confronting other individuals with judgments about performance. As is true of most people, counsellors have a need to be liked by members of the social groups with which they are associated. Counselling can disrupt the personal relationships within such groups. The counsellor often anticipates that this will occur, imagining that the employee will react to the session with hostility, or withdraw during the interview into a shell and thereafter ignore the counsellor's presence except when given direct orders. Such reactions by employees are not uncommon, causing the counsellor to avoid the discussion altogether.

Avoiding the discussion, however, will only

result in the problem and the potential confrontation becoming worse. Counselling is an indispensable aspect. If accomplished effectively, and early at onset of performance problems can resolve problems in a positive manner and ultimately help to strengthen the relationship.

It would be dishonest to assure that there are techniques which will avoid the unpleasant aspects of counselling in every case. Like any aspect of supervision, counselling involves authority over and responsibility for the actions of other employees. It is precisely this authority over others' behaviour that produces the potential conflict, however, such conflict can be *minimized*.

Counsellors considering counselling who are uncertain how to proceed or who face what they believe might be a difficult or sensitive issue should not hesitate to seek advice and assistance from their supervisor or personnel or employee relations office. Understanding how to conduct a counselling session will help supervisors feel confident and calm during that meeting and better prepared to handle conflicts or questions that may arise. There are numerous supervisory training courses available which can provide useful skills and tips for communicating with employees.

When to Conduct Session

There is no hard and fast rule as to when counselling is appropriate. As a general rule counselling is appropriate when the established standards for performance and conduct are not being met. However, the authority must exercise judgment and discretion when determining whether, and at what point, to counsel.

Certain types of behaviour might be a problem after one incident, while others might not become a problem until a pattern develops. For example, an employee who has had excellent attendance for several years may not require counselling due to one day's tardiness. In fact, in such situations, premature attempts at counselling may create a defensive attitude on the part of the employee and negatively impact the employee's job performance. In other circumstances, however, the severity of a situation might warrant counselling following one incident, regardless of the employee's work history.

Determining whether counselling is appropriate in a particular situation requires that the authority carefully review the facts. Factors which the authority should consider in making such determinations include the severity of the incident or behaviour and the impact it has on the workplace, the employee's work history, and, if available, the circumstances surrounding the incident or behaviour. If, after a review and analysis of the available information, the authority continues to be concerned or have questions about the employee's conduct, behaviour, or poor work performance, counselling is both necessary and appropriate. Authority is encouraged to consult with their personnel or employee relations offices for guidance.

Once the authority has determined that counselling is appropriate, it should be conducted promptly. This is important for several reasons. First, it is best to discuss an incident when it is still fresh in the mind of the employee. If the discussion is delayed, specific details of the incident may fade from memory and result in the discussion focusing only on what happened, rather than on why it happened and what corrective measures will be taken. Second, failure to act promptly may give tacit approval to the employee's behaviour, thereby, encouraging the behaviour to continue. Finally, an employee is more likely to question the importance of the matter if the counselling session is conducted long after the incident. In addition to minimizing the effectiveness of the counselling, this may cause the employee to be suspicious of motive in conducting the counselling and increase the potential for conflict.

Procedure

When conducting a counselling session, there are several guidelines one should follow in order to minimize the potential conflict. Most importantly one should not view the session as an opportunity to scold the employee or as a means to threaten the employee with disciplinary action. The purpose is not to punish or reprimand someone, but to determine the cause of the circumstances about which one is concerned. In this light, one should view counselling as a problem-solving exercise. For example: If the employee has been tardy, what prevents the employee from arriving at work on time? How can the employee remedy the problem? In this respect, it is the counsellor's job to set the tone of the meeting, putting the employee at ease as much as possible.

Certainly, where an employee's performance has consistently fallen below standards, it may be necessary for one to advise the employee that failure to respond to the counselling and perform adequately may result in disciplinary action.

Additionally, there are a number of other guidelines which are helpful to understand when counselling employees.

1. *Be prepared*. Spend time reviewing the facts and defining one's objective for the session. One may find it useful to prepare a set of "talking points" in advance to help one be clear about the issues and

point one wishes to make. These talking points do not become the counselling memo.

2. *Counselling session should always be conducted in private.* If you have an office, perhaps that is the best place to schedule the meeting. If not, you should seek another private room away from an employee's co-workers or the people being served by the agency. Failure to provide a private surrounding is likely to create a feeling of humiliation for the employee, which may manifest itself in more, rather than fewer, violations of rules.

3. *Never schedule a counselling session with an employee when you are rushed with other duties.* It will leave the impression that your concern is minimal if you are frequently interrupted, must constantly look at your watch, or you rush the employee out after only a few minutes and before your discussion is complete.

4. When an employee enters your office, *act in a manner consistent with your normal demeanor.* If you are normally relaxed with an employee, be yourself. Otherwise, the employee will believe that the discussion implies a personal conflict. This should be avoided.

5. *Consider setting ground rules.* For example, tell the employee that you are hoping for a conversation to work out the issue. You may say something like "Please hear me out without interruptions, and then I will listen to you and your point of view without interrupting you." If it is true, let the employee know you expect to be able to resolve the issue in a positive way.

6. *Be direct and candid.* After greeting and making the

employee comfortable, go directly to the reason for the meeting. Do not make "small talk". Avoid chatting or asking general question like, "Anything interesting happen today?" Questions such as these simply make employees suspicious of your motives.

7. In broaching the issue(s), you should *explain the exact nature of your concern*, making clear what has been observed and why it is important. For example, you might say: "I received a report today that you were rude to two customers. Obviously, the report concerns me. I want to take this opportunity to discuss the report with you and hear from you what happened." If you already know the names of the two customers involved, you might have added that to the introductory remarks. You should present your concerns directly and openly to the employee.

8. *Where employees are cooperative, your job will be confined to determining what the employee's view of the incidence is.* For example, if the employee responded to your statement, by saying, "Yes, that is true," you should follow-up by asking: "Could you give me the details from your point of view? How did this come about?"

9. *Some employees may be hostile. In those cases, you should remain calm, speaking in measured voice.* Because someone yells at you, it does not mean that you must yell back. You are the counsellor and to control the meeting you must control your emotions and reactions. Rather than reacting to the employee's hostility, you should redirect the employee's attention to your concern: "What occurred in the incident or issue being discussed?" "Why did it happen?" "How can we improve performance to

ensure it does not happen again?" If the employee continues to behave in a hostile or abusive manner toward you, you should calmly advise the employee that such behaviour may result in disciplinary action. If the behaviour continues, you should halt the session and discuss the matter with the employee relations or personnel office. It should be noted that merely disagreeing with the facts as presented is not necessarily hostile behaviour on the part of the employee.

10. *Focus on the behaviour of the employee, not the employee's "character" or "morality."* An employee is more likely to understand that he or she has behaved incorrectly in a particular circumstance than to accept a supervisor's assertion that his or her basic character is unacceptable. For example, it is appropriate to say, "Your behaviour on the ward today was rude," but it is never appropriate to say, "You are a rude person."

11. *Be a good listener.* Give the employee the opportunity to explain his or her version of the incident or circumstances about which you are concerned. Don't interrupt the employee while they are talking.

12. *Keep an open mind* during the counselling session. If the discussion raises a question or reveals that your information was incorrect, or the employee's explanation is satisfactory, say so to the employee. Even where the employee's explanation is not satisfactory, the employee is more likely to accept your judgment if you have given him or her the opportunity to explain.

13. In listening to the employee's version of the incidents, a number of possible explanations may

emerge. *After hearing the employee's explanation, you must decide whether other actions may be appropriate in addition to reinforcing to the employee what the rules are.* For example, the employee may need additional training, or perhaps reassignment so a supervisor can give closer instruction. You may not wish to make those decisions at the time of the counselling, but ask to see the employee at a later date after you have considered the options.

14. If the employee indicates that the problem is personal, or if you have some indication that the problem is other than work related, *tell the employee about available assistance, such as the Employee Assistance Program (EAP).*

15. *Reach an understanding* on the corrective action which will be taken and set a definite follow-up date.

16. At the conclusion of the counselling session, you should thank the employee for seeing you and extend yourself to the employee should further problems of this nature arise. *Ultimately you want the employee to know that you are available to assist in solving such problems* before they erupt into the types of incidents which prompted the counselling session.

17. *If you intend to confirm the session in writing, inform the employee that you intend to write a counselling memo and that a copy will be placed in their personnel file.*

The Counselling Memo

In some instances, the counsellor may feel it is appropriate or necessary to formalize the counselling session with a memo. As with the counselling session, there are no definitive rules as to when it is appropriate to issue a counselling memo. Each case must be handled individually and a determination made based on the facts and circumstances surrounding the case.

Prior to issuing a counselling memo, the counsellor should carefully consider the need for such action. For most persons the written record may represent a higher level of conflict than the actual interview. Many employees will become defensive upon receiving one. Therefore, it is best to reserve sending memos for those situations which warrant it.

Generally, a memo is both appropriate and necessary when:
1) Previous counselling has failed to result in improvement
2) You do not have confidence that the employee will correct the improper behaviour without further encouragement
3) The seriousness of the situation requires documentation that the session was held
4) A multi-part plan for improvement was discussed during the session and the memo serves as written conformation and a reminder of the plan or to document specific instructions given to the employee during the session.

If at the end of the counselling session you have determined that a counselling memo is necessary, you should tell the employee of your decision before concluding the session. Giving the employee such notice can help to blunt a hostile reaction, at least to the extent that the employee is not surprised by the written summary.

When a counselling memo is sent, it should be sent as close to the counselling session as possible. Otherwise, both the supervisor and the employee are likely to forget important aspects of the discussion. Additionally, the purpose in sending the memo is to reinforce understandings reached during the counselling session, it is also widely accepted that such learning takes place more effectively when the reinforcement (i.e., the memo) is close to the initial event (i.e., counselling session).

Writing a Counselling Memo

In several ways, writing a counselling memo is not dissimilar from conducting the counselling session itself. First, a counselling memo is a summary of the counselling session which should be addressed and delivered (or sent) to the employee. Second, the memo should be similar in tone to the session. It should not be punitive. In this respect, it should not be characterized as a disciplinary notice or letter of reprimand, it is neither.

When writing a counselling memo, the following guidelines should be followed:

1. Write the memo to the employee
2. Be concise and clear
3. The memo is a summary of your counselling session. Include the following sections:
   a. A statement of the reason for and the date, time, and place of the meeting. Be as complete as possible in describing the problem.
   b. The employee's response to your concerns. This is important as it demonstrates to the employee that you were actually listening during the counselling session.
   c. The manner in which the employee is expected to improve performance. Also clearly provide

your expectations for future performance or behaviour.

d. Provisions for follow-up consultations, if any.

e. If situation warrants, recommend Employee Assistance Program to employee to handle personal problem interfering with work performance or behaviour.

f. Do not include other matters in the memo which were not discussed during the session.

4. Do not characterize the memo as discipline or as a penalty.

5. The tone of the memo should be supportive and factual. Avoid labels or conclusive language. Do not write it in a punitive or derogatory manner. Avoid inflammatory language.

Chapter : 11

Skills in Counselling

The process of employee counselling is a complex phenomenon. It has several dimensions. However, an important dimension is the skill of the counsellor. While a number of skills are important, the basic ingredient involves listening and communication skills.

Listening Skills

Have you had the experience of listening to a lecture only to realize you remember nothing that has been said? You may have *heard* it, but you weren't *listening*. The process by which we make sense of what we hear is **listening**. There is a distinction between hearing the words and really listening to the message. Hearing alone is not listening. Hearing only means that you recognize that a message is being sent – you may or may not be listening the information in the message and trying to reach a common understanding between you and the sender of the message.

By becoming a better listener, you will improve your effectiveness and knowledge base as well as your ability to influence, persuade and counsell. You would also avoid conflict and misunderstanding – all worthy goals for a counsellor.

Barriers to Listening

Listening involves mentally participating in a conversation for the purpose of comprehending what the speaker is communicating. This is especially true in counselling, where counsellors are expected to exhibit effective listening skills. Unfortunately, many roadblocks or barriers can prevent counselling from comprehending. Some of the barriers can be identified.

Distractions. You cannot allow yourself to be distracted by what is going on around you. When you are trying to listen to a client, someone whispering nearby breaks your train of thought. Similarly, someone giving you directions or a phone ringing nearby diverts your attention. You may also be distracted by the unusual dress of a client, a mispronounced word, or an unusual voice quality or dialect. These distractions can easily steal your thoughts away from the client.

Thinking ahead. In a conversation, people take turns speaking and listening. Unfortunately, sometimes instead of listening people think about what they will say next. When this happens, you are hearing but not listening. You reply may not make sense because you did not listen to all the words of the speaker. Perhaps the conversation moved to a new topic and you missed it.

Mind moving too fast. People can think faster than they can speak. Most speakers talk at a rate of about 120 to 150 words per minute. Most receivers listen and think at a rate of exceeding 1000 words a minute. If you are listening at a rate of 1000 words per minute, your thoughts can wonder ahead of the speaker while you are listening. You may begin to daydream, think about what you need to do later, or wonder what your friends are doing. When this happens, you miss the points the speaker is making because your mind is elsewhere and you are no longer focused on the speaker.

Lack of attention. Too often when someone is talking we don't listen attentively. Good listening requires keeping one's thoughts on what is being said. Paying attention will prevent you from missing important information. For example, if you are being given direction on an important matter, you may do something wrong and you may create problem for you.

Selective attention. Selective listening means hearing only what you want to hear. If means "turning out" someone who is trying to make a point.

It is a common characteristic to skip over the uncomfortable, the unpleasant, or the difficult and comprehend only part of a message. This may happen when you hear something that conflicts with your personal thoughts, beliefs, or convictions. Or you may be selective when you receive information that you don't want to hear or that is simply being presented at an inconvenient time. Selective listening is not an option in the counselling. You must pay careful attention to everything being said.

Active Listening

You spend more time listening that speaking, reading or writing. Yet listening remains one of the least understood and least studied part of communication process. Listening is an art that needs to be practiced and perfected.

If you want to improve your listening skill, your goal should be to become an "**active listener**". An active listener makes a conscious effort to hear not only words that another person is saying to you but more importantly to try and understand the total message being sent. Active listening requires concentration and determination on the part of the listener. While active listening, the receiver sends the speaker's message back to the speaker (sender) for verification. If the misunderstanding has occurred, it will be known immediately, and communication can be clarified.

These are other benefits to active listening. Active listening can clarify points of agreement so that the areas of disagreement are put in perspective and diminished. There are a few other tips.

Prepare to listen. Your efficiency as listener improves if you prepare yourself mentally and physically to listen. Block out miscellaneous thoughts that are running through your mind. Try to erase competing thoughts. You cannot act on these thoughts now, so push them aside and prepare to listen. Focus on what is being said and block out what is not important at the time.

An active listener acts like a good listener. Sit or stand in a way that is comfortable. Face the speaker and be alert. Your body position defines whether you are an active listener. Look directly at the speaker. A visual bond between speaker and listener is effortant for effective listening. Your eyes will complete the communication circuit that must be established between speaker and listener. When we focus attention on the speaker and what is being said, you reinforce what you are hearing. Active listening means accepting 100 percent responsibility by receiving the same message that the speaker sent, uncontaminated by your own thoughts or feelings. The process of jolting down key points strengthening your listening skill.

Avoid emotional response. An open mind is a must for active listening. Control your emotional responses to the speaker's message. Sometimes client's words trigger emotional responses – positive or negative. Poor listeners spend time responding "red flag" words and frequently miss the message.

Separate fact from opinion. In many situations, it is necessary to separate facts from the opinion of clients. This is called **critical listening**. A critical listening determines the accuracy of the message. A **fact** is information that can be proven. An **opinion** is based on personal beliefs or feelings. Critical listening is important when clients express their opinions as fact. You must evaluate each message to decide what is fact and what is opinion.

Communication in Counselling

Communication involves transmission of stimuli and evocation of responses. In other words, communication is a measure of 'one – mindedness', a sharing of the same thought and feeling. A message is communicated only if the reception is accurate. It is a case of becoming "like-minded".

Linear Model of Communication

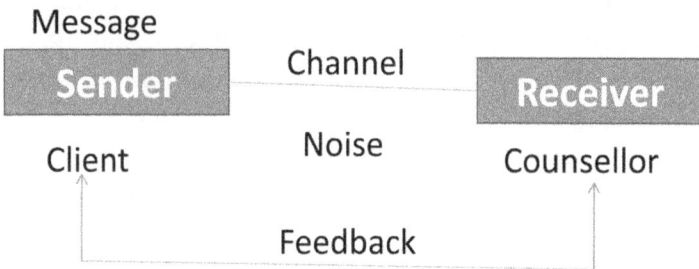

Linear Model of Communication

Message

| Sender | Channel | Receiver |
| Client | Noise | Counsellor |

Feedback

Communication is a "social process". The verbal, non-verbal, and body language aspects of communication have been discussed in many contexts. An important element in communication network involves **channel**. Scheflen has outlined channels as language modalities and non-language modalities. Language modalities include (a) linguistics, including lexical, stress, pitch, and junctures, and (b) paralinguistics, including non language sounds and vocal modifiers. Non-language modalities include (a) Kinesics and postural, including voluntary and involuntary behaviour, facial expression, tonus, positioning, (b) tactile, (c) odorifies, (d) proxemics, and (e) artifactual including dress, cosmetic usuage and décor.

All communication coveys both content and relationship. It is found that **while words can be used to communicate almost anything, relationship is communicated primarily by paralinguistic and nonlanguage modalities**. Someone may wish to communicate to you the fat that he/she wishes the door closed, but how this is conveyed to you, the potential door-closer, may well define the relationship between you. Your mode of response, verbal and nonverbal, will further clarify this relationship. If you respond by slamming the door shut, you are conveying a different message than if you were to close it gently. This implies that communication consists of both content and relationship definition.

In counselling, the client is communicating more than she/he is aware of. In effective counselling, the attempt is to move to a level at which this communication is understood.

Further understanding of, communication process is possible by examining different types of communication patterns of the client.

Types of Communication

There are various categories of communication patterns in the client.

The noncommunicative person. The noncommunicative person focuses on his/her own words to say only what he/she thinks or what he/she wants to say. He or she does not take the listener into consideration. In counselling, this defensiveness has to be broken.

Overly logical speaker. Some individuals have a need to be precise and accurate in what they say. This, of course, reaches its most exaggerated form in obsessive personality.

Under talker. Because of fear of disclosure, some individuals make understatement. This is a form of self-protectiveness arising from a sense of inadequacy.

Over talker. The over talker is typically not a listener. He/she may be basically an anxious insecure person. Great verbal output does not necessarily mean, however, that the individual is revealing a great deal of information about himself/herself.

Tangential speaker. The tangential speaker counters the other person's statements by throwing in side remarks and irrelevancies. The power and control-oriented individual may use it to disrupt someone else's communication.

Helpless speaker. This individual presents the picture of someone seeking for help, but the request is often accompanied by an accusation that the other person is either incapable or unwilling to fulfill it.

While an individual may fall typically into one of these communication patterns, one person may use several of them at different times and in various situations.

Interpersonal Relation in Counselling

Personal growth is facilitated when the counsellor in the relationship with his/her client is genuine and without "front" or faced. There are several conditions that define such relationship.

Congruence. It is hypothesized that the more genuine and congruent the therapy is in the relationship the more probably that change in the client will occur. It is important that the counsellor is deep and true, not superficial. The word transparency helps to describe the element of personal congruence.

Empathy. It is needed that the counsellor experiences an accurate empathetic understanding of the client's private world and is able to communicate some of the significant aspects of that understanding.

Positive regard. Growth and change are more likely to occur when the counsellor expresses a warm, positive, acceptant attitude towards the client. It means that he/she values his/her client as a person, with somewhat same kind of feeling that a parent feels towards his/her child.

Chapter : 12

Effective Interviewing

Interviewing clients is an integral component of the counselling process. A skilled counsellor needs to have appropriate interviewing skills to establish rapport with the client. It is also needed to identify problems to monitor the progress and facilitate adaptive changes in clients. The interaction between the counsellor and the client, like any other human interaction, gives out a complex variety of stimuli. The para-verbal cues, non-verbal cues and verbal statements provide a rich multitude of stimuli which may help or hurt the counselling process. A skilled counsellor makes positive use of these ingradients and reduces the hindering effects of negative elements.

The major dimensions of attending skills include attending skills and influencing skills.

Attending Skills

Attending behaviour is the central aspect of counselling process. It involves four key elements: eye contact, appropriate body language, vocal tone and verbal behaviour. The principle of *selective attention* posits that the counsellor has to selectively attend to verbal and non-verbal cues provided by the client. At the same time, the counsellor has to ignore some aspects of clients' statements.

It is important to recognize that the process of selective attention (what to select and what to ignore) depends on the specific orientation of the counsellor. For example, a psychoanalytically oriented counsellor, would be more attentive to clients' narrative describing his or her past interactions and memories. The early experiences described by the client would be stressed. A behaviouristically oriented counsellor would pay greater attention to situational parameters and concrete behaviours. A counsellor with cognitive orientation would be inclined to look for clients' belief statements.

In order to interview or counsel clients, it seems that counsellorsshould look naturally at the clients. The avoidance of eye contact may indicate the lack of interest whereas the fixation of the gaze may control client's expression. Sigmund Freud never used to stand infront of the alien, he used to stand behind a chair in which the client is seated. The natural eye movement appears to be appropriate during counselling session.

In the past the verbal contents were considered only ingradients in counselling interview. Presently this is not a tenable belief. Both *para-verbal behaviour* and *non-verbal components* are considered important. An appropriate use of these cues enhances the process of attention.

Para-verbal Contents. A number of features of spoken language changes the nature of speech. The speed of saying something, the pitch, the tone, loudness and intonation constitute the para-verbal elements. Some people are slow speakers while others are fast speakers. Generally we speak 100 to 150 words per minute while the mind processes 400 to 500 words per minute. We may surmise the advantages and disadvantages of slow speaking versus fast speaking. If the counsellor speaks too fast, the client may miss some of the words. If the counsellor speaks very slow there is also a problem. While listening the client may develop counter-attitudinal thoughts. For example, the counsellor advises to give up smoking. Yet the client may use inner speech (within the time gap) that many smokers have achieved tremendous success in their lives. These intervening thoughts may forestall the change process desired by the counsellor. Hence it is appropriate to use a moderate pace of speaking. However, intonation has to be varied. The goal of saying something personal and intimate may have a specific style while the objective of commanding something would have different style. The para-verbal cues are very helpful in establishing rapport, displaying counsellor's interest and commitment.

Non-verbal Communication. In communication scenarios, the following four types of non-verbal elements are used:

1. *Para-linguistic cues* (body language) involving inter-personal distance, touch, gestures, hand movement, body movement, eye glances
2. *Artifactual cues:* dress, cosmetics, hair style
3. *Mediational cues*: Use of media such as newspaper, TV, and radio
4. *Contextual cues*: Structuring of time and space.

The body language component is very important. The *interpersonal distance* (technically called *proxemics*) conveys a lot of things. It denotes closeness via-a-vis distance. Too much distance from the client may indicate a lack of distance. At the other extreme, too much closeness may denote interference. A judicious amount of interpersonal space would convey counsellor's interest in the welfare of the client. However, the appropriateness of distance depends on the specific context of the conversation as well as cultural parameters. While discussing an intimate topic, the counsellor may lean forward to reduce the physical distance. Similarly, distance may be adjusted when a male counsellor is talking with a female client. Other paralinguistic cues such as touch, hand movement are guided by cultural norms. As indicated earlier, normal eye glance appears to be fine. The client may not feel that he or she is under a scanner.

The use of artifactual cues depends on the context. Some organizations do have their dress code. The manipulation of these cues are guided by the factors of climate setting. However, the formal setting of counselling would require some specification. The use of mediational cues demands wise decisions. If the counsellor is talking with the client and gleaning through the pages of a book or magazine, it would convey the lack of interest on the part of the counsellor. This should be avoided. However, the counsellor may open the pages of a book to indicate "the session is over, you may please go". Thus, the use signals the end of the session. Finally, the contextual cues involve the structuring of time and place. If he session is arranged during working hours, it implies that the things would go in a formal way.If arranged otherwise, it means that there is a mix of formal and informal talks. Similarly, sitting arrangement also carries some implications. The proportion of formal versus informal interaction, the primacy of the speaker (whether or not the client would speak to most) are signaled by the sitting arrangement. On the whole, the non-verbal elements play decisive role in gearing the course of verbal interactions.

In addition, the following tips may be employed:
- Body should communicate interest.
- Voice should indicate interest in listening.
- Topics must not be changed abruptly.

Microskills of Attending

Attending behaviour entails a number of microskills on the part of the counsellor. A skilled counsellor makes use of these skills to ensure clients' rapport, attentiveness, listening interest and compliance.

Open Questions. Counsellors may use open questions toobtain information from clients. These questions generally begin with "What"., "Why", "When" and "Where". Clients in response to these questions ae likely to provide longer, more informative sentences. This is in sharp contrast to closed questions where clients answer either in affirmative or in negative. The counsellor may use a number of open questions to obtain detailed account.

Closed Questions. While open questions generate long answers, closed questions serve some purpose. When clients ae speechless, closed questions may be used at least in the beginning, to open windows. Once clients become verbal, subsequent use of open question serve helpful purpose. A representative sample of closed questions include the following:

- Are you feeling fine?
- Do you often feel tired?
- Would you like to visit new places?
- Are you comfortable with strangers?

Encouragers and Restatements. Encouragers and restatements are active ways of letting clients know that they are heard and they can go on. Encouragers and restatements offer the least intrusions into the client's world.

Paraphrases. These are concise repetitions of the clients' main words and thoughts. Selective attention is given to objective content of the client's expressions.

Summarization. The gathering together of a client's verbalizations, facts, feelings and meanings and presenting them to the client is useful. It provides a pause to the interview.

Influencing Skills
The influencing skill is complex and it involves a number of components.

Interpretation. The skilled counsellor is likely to interpret the dynamics of the problem on basis of the interview and generate some inferences.

Directives. Directives are the statements that counsellors direct towards the clients. Clients are asked to do certain things, practice certain ways and follow specific advice.

Information. A set of useful information is provided to clients. Therapist train clients in the direction of complying with the information. Periodic feedback is obtained from clients to monitor the progress of counselling.

Integrating Positive Skills
Counselling is a remedial process in which the task is to shape the worldview of the client. It is concerned with restructuring adaptive thought patterns, repeating patterns of faulty behaviour comes from childhood learning. These may also come from recent traumas of living. The objective of both counselling and psychotherapy is change the faulty patterns. In a such a scheme of adaptive changes, positive assets and skills are to be acquired and practiced. In addition to counselling support system provided by family, workgroups, community centres is considered vital. A number of support systems help in integrating the positive skills and make it a moredurableand tangible change in to afflicted client.

Part 2:
Additional Tools and Techniques

Chapter : 13

Transactional Analysis

Eric Berne is usually credited with having started the Transactional Analysis (TA) movement with his best selling book Games People Play, and Thomas Harris's book I'm OK – You're OK further popularized TA. Other books by James ad Jongeward are more relevant to organizational applications. TA is very popular today and has a wide appeal. In many respect, it is confused with the equally popular transcendental meditation (TM) movement. However, TA's popularity lies in its use of understandable everyday relevant terminology. Everyone can readily relate to the concepts and practices of TA.

In an organizational change programme, TA is often intended to help the organization members in several ways:

1. Improve interpersonal communication.
2. Develop improved ways and styles for managing interpersonal conflicts.
3. Gain self-insight by becoming more aware of their own behaviour and obtaining feedback from others.
4. Develop diagnostic skills, particularly as related to the individual and small groups.
5. Acquire an understanding of the factors that interfere with or facilitate group functioning.
6. Reduce self-defecting attitudes and behaviours.

TA was first formally developed by Berne in 1961 and was elaborated by in a number of succeeding books.

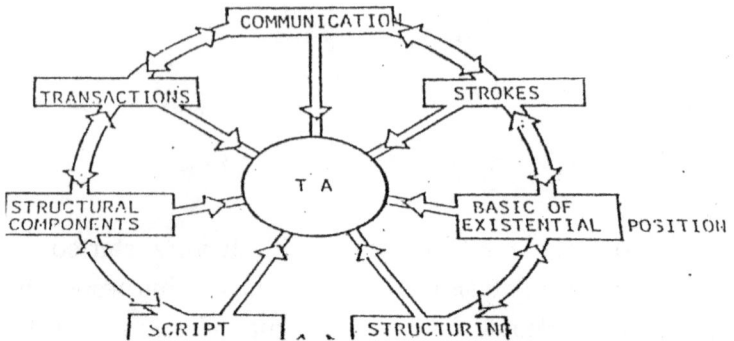

BASIC ELEMENTS IN TRANSACTIONAL ANALYSIS

As shown in the Figure, the basic model consists of seven independent elements : Structural components, transaction, contamination, strokes, basic or existential position, structuring of time, and script analysis.

Structural Components

The structural components of the TA model are three ego state: Parent, Adult, and Child. An ego state is the typical way of feeling, thinking, and reacting. Each of us is capable of displaying these three ego states.

The Parent ego state is the felling, thoughts, and reactions in each of us that ae similar to those perceived by us in our mothers, fathers, or other important individuals who might have reared us. The parent in us assumes numerous functions, including setting limits, giving advice, disciplining, guiding, protecting, making rules and regulations about how life should be (the musts, shoulds, always, nevers, goods, bads, etc.). it also functions to teach is how to keep tradition, nature, judge, and criticize. In themselves, the parental functions, like those of the other ego states, are not necessarily to be regarded as good or bad. One of the objectives of the TA change approach is to assist us in becoming more aware of its Parent ego state and them to help each of us determine for ourselves what forms and posts of it are relevant or irrelevant to our current lives. This is to help us live our own lives and not those of our parents.

The Adult ego state is the part that computes, stores experiences and uses facts to make decisions. The adult ego state is to unemotional knowledge part of us. In the TA model, the Adult ego is not intended to mean or suggest maturity. The Adult functions include data gathering on these three ego states, identifying and assessing alternatives, setting objectives and determining how to attain them, and all components of ordered planning and the decision-making process.

The Child ego state is what we were in our younger years. There could be a number of "Children" in us from the past. The child is us could range from angry, rebellious, frightened, or conforming to creative, carefree, fun loving, adventurous, and trusting.

All of these ego states exist within us, and all are important. It is desirable to have our Adult operating at all times so that it can keep us aware of the parent and the child and the situation.

Transactions

Transactions are interactions we have with others and with our internal selves. Transactions include verbal and nonverbal communications that vary from an exchange of compliments to a brawl. The three basic forms of transactions are: parallel, crossed, and ulterior.

Parallel Transaction

Transactions are parallel when the lines of communication between two individuals are complementary, such as Parent to and from Parent, Parent to and from Child, and Parent to and from Adult.

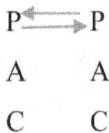  

1. Parent – Parent Transaction
   Manager   : An effective maintenance repair program always reduces cost.
   Employee : I always say that a stich in time saves nine.
2. Parent – Child Transaction
   Manager   : An effective maintenance repair program always reduces cost.
   Employee : Yes, Sir
3. Parent – Adult Transaction
   Manager   : An effective maintenance repair program always reduces cost.
   Employee : The problem is the new supplier. Maintenance record shows that his parts do not last as do the parts from the Stars Company.

In these examples and the Figure, the transactions are parallel.

Crossed Transaction

A non-complementary crossed transaction occurs when the interactions do not have common origination and terminal ego states. Difficulties in communications and arguments often arise from crossed transactions.

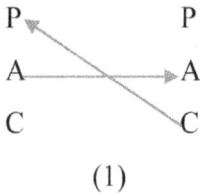

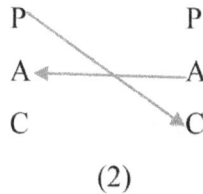

```
P            P              P            P
 \                           \
A ———————→ A              A ←——————— A
 \                           \
C          C              C          C
   (1)                       (2)
```

1. Crossed Transaction

   Ravi   : Do you know how it takes to get to New Delhi?

   Joten   : I wish we could stop for refreshment.

2. Crossed Transaction

   Manager   : You can never trust machines. Sometimes they go wrong.

   Employee : You can't blame machine for your lack of expertise.

Ulterior Transaction

Ulterior transactions occur when one individual attempts to create the impression of relating to one ego state when, infact, he or she is responding to another. Ulterior transactions are attempts to be dishonest, manipulate, or engage in unconscious "game playing". Ulterior transaction involves the simultaneous activity of more than two egos and on the basis for psychological games. An example is given :

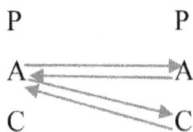

(1)

1. Ulterior Transaction
   Ravi   : you'd get a better TV for another Rs. 500/-,
   but I don't think you can afford it.
   Mohan   : I'll take it.

Here Ravi the sales person behaves Adult-Adult on the social level, but Adult-Child on the psychological level. This is done with the hope of hooking the child into responding "yes, I'll take it". A wary Adult would realize the financial responsibility and smash the offer.

Contamination

Contamination is the child's acceptance in us of our parents' prejudices, opinions, and feelings as our own. Thus, we may be prone not to use our Adult to check out the facts for ourselves.

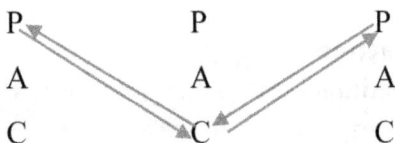

(1)

1. Contamination Transaction
   Father: Rina, let me warn you that you can never trust managers, they are no good and only try to exploit you.

Grandfather: That's right, Rina. This family is proud of its tradition

Rina   : Ok.

Strokes

TA experts feel that every one has to have strokes. Using the common definition of the word, this means simply that beginning in infancy and continuing throughout their lives, people need cuddling, affection, recognition, and praise. Not every one is turned on by same strokes, (in the vernacular of TA this is stated as "different strokes for different folks"). But every one needs them. It may be a simple "good morning", or a pat on the back every once in a while.

Strokes may be either positive, negative or mixed. Positive strokes feel good when they are received, and contribute to a person's sense of being OK. Negative strokes hurt physically or emotionally and make us feel less OK about ourselves. An example of a mixed stroke is the supervisor's comment, "Dillip, that's a good advertising layout, considering the small amount of experience you have in this field".

There is also a difference between conditional and unconditional strokes. Conditional strokes are offered to employees if they perform correctly and avoid problems. A sales manager may promise that "I will give you a raise if you sell three more insurance policies". Unconditional strokes are presented without any correction to behaviour. Supervisor will get better results if they link the reward to the desired activity.

Life Positions

Each person tends to exhibit one of four life positions, very early in childhood a person develops a dominant way of relating to people. That philosophy tends to remain with the person for a life time unless major experiences occur to change it. This is called basic or existential life position.

Life positions stem from a combination of two view points, as shown in the Figure. First, how do people view themselves? Second, how do they view other people in general?

		I'm Ok You're not OK	I'm Ok – You're OK
Attitude towards self	Positive		
	Negative	I'm not OK- You're not OK	I'm not OK- You're OK
		Negative	Positive

Attitude towards other

These positions can be described as follows:
1. **I'm O.K. You're O.K.** This is the healthing position that is the ultimate change objective in transactional analysis.
2. **I'm O.K. You're not O.K.** This is a position of distrust in which the child in us is suspicious of other people.
3. **I'm not O.K. You're O.K.** In this position the child in us has a negative self-concept and is likely to feel depressed.
4. **I'm not O.K. You're no O.K.** In this position, the child in us feels that other people, itself, and life in general "just aren't any good". At the extremes of this position, the child could sense total helplessness or rage and possibly engage in suicide or homicide.

The desirable position and that one involves the greatest likelihood of Adult to Adult transaction is "I'm OK – You're OK". It shows healthy acceptance of self and others. That other three life positions are less psychologically mature and less effective. The important point is that.

regardless of one's present life position, the "I'm OK – You're OK" position can be learned. There is lies organization's hope for improved interpersonal transactions.

Structuring of Time

Our basic position will influence how we structure our time. Six types of time structuring are expressed through transactions: withdrawal, rituals, activities, pastimes, games, and intimely. Withdrawal is the psychological removal of ourselves from the people around us, as for example by constantly day dreaming. Rituals are transactions that are socially agreed upon ways of behaving towards each other. Activities are spontaneous transactions between or among individuals such as eating, playing tennis, and working. Pastimes are transactions that serve to full time with others, such as discussing Sunday's cricket match and gossiping.

Of all these, games people play are very relevant to some of the things that go in modern organizations.

Games Managers Play

One version of TA has been popularized by Webber as games managers play. Webber says that people often slip into certain roles or ego state. Understanding one's own "role" (and that of the person one is speaking to) can help a manager understand the motives underlying what he (and the person he is speaking with) is saying. Versions of roles include persecutor, rescuer and victim.

Persecutors seem driven to manipulate others to feel badly through blame, ridiculing, bulling, criticizing, belittling, threatening, and so on. These verbal abuses are often accompanied by an accusingly pointed finger. Two specific games people play include now I've got you and blemish.

The "now I've got you" managers try to make others feel bad to cover up his or her own negative feelings. These persons criticize others excessively whenever they violate his or her standards. The "now I have got you" managers behave this way partly because they want to escape their underlying feelings of low self-esteem. It can be avoided by providing clear and achievable standards and by making available the information and resources needed to succeed. The "blemish" players on the other hand criticize insignificant flaws in performance rather than regarding major success. He or she persecutes by constantly finding minor gaps in logic rather than trying to understand the bigger picture. Blemish players seem driven by an uncontrollable need to correct and find fault with others.

Victim players continue blame, procrastinate, make mistakes and apologize in order to manipulate others to "rescue" or "persecute" him. Unlike a real victim, the helplessness of the person is imaginary. Victims use language like "I have tried everything", "I don't know", and "I can't do it" accompanied by dejected postures and helpless facial expression. The things that often keep the victim going are the negative strokes they receive.

Rescuers like to meddle in other's decisions, give unsolicited advice, or not let subordinates carry their share of the work load. Their favourite phrases include: "I would love to do it for you". "If I were you, I'd". People who receive a rescuer's unwanted advice can usually stop this game by telling the person that they will ask for help when they need it. Manager rescuers thus have to guard against alienating competent subordinates with their unwanted advice.

Games, thus, are a set of transactions, often repetitious, superficially plausible, with a concealed motivation. The outcome of games is almost always a win-lose proposition. Games are dysfunctional for productive interpersonal relations and detract from organizational effectiveness. The goal should be to create an organizational climate that does not need or tolerate game playing.

In contrast, intimacy as a form of time structuring involves transactions concerned with the mutuality of two or more people in a shared identity. Mutuality occurs through giving, sharing, taking risks, and trusting one another.

Script Analysis

Our script is the life plan we feel compelled to act out. It is closely related to our basic position and our way of structuring time. A script is thought to be a subconscious life-plan formed within our child by early period of our life. Although decisions have been made about our script at one point of time, it can be redecided. Individuals with problems often have scripts with unfavourable outcomes (sickness, failure, insanity). One of the aims of TA is to assist us in freeing ourselves from these scripts.

Final Comments

When supervisors transact primarily from the single ego state, they limit their choice of leadership style. For example, the person with a dominant parent ego state will tend towards a more autocratic style. If the child state is dominant, the free-rein style may be used extensively. However, a supervisor who feels "I'm OK – You're OK" and has a well-developed Adult state is more likely to collect data prior to making a choice of style. The style chosen by the Adult state generally will allow ample freedom for employee to participate.

TA offers fresh insights into individuals' own personalities and help them understand what they really can do to improve. Employees can sense when crossed communications occur and then can take steps to restore complementary communication, preferably in the Adult-to-Adult pattern. The result is a general improvement in interpersonal transactions.

Chapter : 14

Alternative Models of Counselling

Effective counselling incorporate a wide range of models and procedures. Much depends on the purpose of counselling the setting the personality and style of the counsellor, the qualities of the particular client and the problems selected for intervention. Regardless of the counselling model, the counsellor must decide what relationship style to adopt, *what* techniques, procedures or intervention methods to use, *when* to use them, and with *which* clients. It is critical to be aware of how clients' cultural backgrounds contribute to their perceptions of their problems. Each of the models has both strengths and limitations.

While a number of principal models are presented a few other additional alternatives may enrich the workable tools.

Gestalt Model

Frederick ("Fritz") Perls (1893 – 1970) was the main originator and developer of Gestalt model. Born in Berlin (Germany), into a lower-middle-class-Jewish family, he lato identified himself as a source of much trouble for his parents. Although he failed the seventh grade twice and was expelled from school because of difficulties with authorities his brilliance was never quashed and he returned. He completed his school education and earned his medical degree with a specialization in psychiatry in 1916. He joined the German Army and served as a medic in World War I. His experience with soldiers who where gassed on the front lines led to his interest in mental functioning, which led him to gestalt psychology. Later he married Laura and began their collaboration.

Gestalt therapy is an existential phenomenological, and process-based approach created on the premise that individuals must be understood in the context of their ongoing relationship with the environment. Awareness, choice and responsibility are key concepts of practice. The main goal is for clients to expand their awareness of what they are experiencing in the present moment. Through the awareness, change automatically occurs. The approach is phenomenological because it focuses on the client's perception of reality and existential because it is grounded on the notion that people are always in the process of becoming, remaking, and rediscovering themselves.

The gestalt approach stresses dialogue and relationship between the client and the counsellor. It employs a style that is supportive, accepting, empathetic, respectful, as well as challenging. The emphasis is on the quality of the counsellor-client relationship and empathic attunement while tapping the client's wisdom and resources.

Basic Principles

Several basic principles underly the theory of gestalt counselling.

Holism. Gestalt is a German word meaning whole or completion, or a form that cannot be separated into parts without losing the essence. All of nature is seen as aunified and coherent whole. The whole is different from the sum of the parts. Gestalt counsellors are interested in the whole person, they place no special value on a specific aspect of the person.

The Figure-and-Ground Principle. Derived from the study of visual perception, the figure-formation process describes how the individual organizes experiences from moment to moment. In Gestalt counselling the field differentiates into a foreground (figures) and a background (ground). The figure-ground process tacks how some aspect of the environmental field emerges from the background and becomes the focal point of the client's attention and interest. The dominant need of an individual at a given moment influence this process.

Organismic Self-Regulation. This is interwined with figure-and-ground principle. The equilibrium is disturbed by the emergence of a new need. Organisms will do their best to regulate themselves, given their own capabilities and resources of the environment. The gestalt counselling directs the client's awareness to the figures that emerge from the background during counselling session.

The Now. One of the main contributions of gestalt counselling is its emphasis on learning to appreciate and fully experience the present moment. Focusing on the past and the future can be a way to avoid coming to terms with the present. Gestalts believe that "power is in the present". Generally clients invest their energies in bemoaning their past mistakes and engaging in future plans. The gestalt counsellors help clients to use the power of the present.

Interventions and Techniques

Experiments can be useful to help the client to gain full

awareness. The goal is to bring about integrated functioning and acceptance of aspects of one's personality that has been disowned and denied. A number of techniques are used.

The Empty-Chair Technique. It is one way of getting the client to externalize the introject, a technique Perls (Fritz Perl and Laura Perl) used a great deal. Using two chairs the counsellor asks the client to sit in one chair and be fully the top dog and then shift to the other chair and become the underdog. The dialogue can continue between both the sides of the client. Essentially, this is a role-playing technique in which all the parts are played by the client. In this way the introjects can surface, and the client can experience the conflict more fully. The conflict can be resolved by the client's acceptance and integration of both sides.

Making the Rounds. Making the rounds is a gestalt intervention that asks a person to go to a group and either speak or to do something with each person. The purpose is to confront, to risk, to disclose the self to experiment with new behaviour.

The Reversal Exercise. Certain symptoms and behaviours often represent reversals of underlying or latent impulses. The counsellor could ask a person who claims to suffer from severe inhibitions and excessive shyness to play the role of an exhibitionist.

The Rehearsal Exercise. Often we get stuck rehearsing silently to ourselves so that we will gain acceptance. When it comes to performance we experience stage fright or anxiety, because we fear that we will not play our role well. Internal rehearsal consumes much energy and frequently inhibit our spontaneity. When clients share their internal rehearsals loud with the counsellor, they become aware of their limitations.

Gestalt counsellors who have truly integrated their approach are sensitive enough to practice in a flexible way. They consider the client's cultural framework and are able to adapt methods that are likely to be well received. They strive to help clients experience themselves as fully as possible in the present, yet they are not rigidly bound by dictates.

Reality Model

Reality counsellors believe the underlying problem of most clients is the same: they are either involved in a present unsatisfying relationship or lack what could be called a relationship. Many of the problems of client are caused by their inability to contact, to get close to others, or to have a successful relationship with at least one significant person in their lives. The counsellor helps clients towards satisfying relationship and teaches them more effective ways of behaving. The more clients are able to connect with people, the greater chance they have to experience happiness.

William Glasser (2003) contends that clients should not be labeled with a diagnosis. Reality counselling is based on **choice theory** as it is explained in several of Glasser's books. Choice theory is the theoretical basis for reality therapy, it explains why and how we function. Reality theory provides a delivery system for helping individuals to make effective choices to deal with people they need in their lives. Glasser maintains that it is essential for the counsellor to establish a satisfying relationship with clients as a prerequisite for effective counselling. Once this relationship is developed the skill of the counsellor as a teacher assumes central role.

The WDEP system can be used to help clients in

reality counselling. Each of the letters refers to a cluster of strategies: W = Wants, needs, and perceptions, D = direction and doing, E = self-evaluation, and P = planning.

Reality counsellors assist clients in discovering their wants, needs and hopes. The key question asked is: "What do you want?" The focus on the present is characterized by the reality counsellor: "What are you doing?" Early in counselling it is essential to discuss with clients the overall directions of their lives. Self-evaluation forms a key element. The counsellor taps this when he/she asks: Is your current behaviour bringing you closer to people you value and closer to the needs you pursue? The key question "What is your plan" is also a seminal step.

The core principles of choice theory and reality counselling are instrumental in strengthening the reality appraisals on the part of the clients. However, some reality therapists may make the mistake of too quickly or too forcefully stressing the ability of their clients to take change of their lives.

Solution – Focused Brief Counselling

Solution – focused brief counselling (SFBC) is a future focused, goal-oriented model developed initially by StiveShazer and Insor Kim Berg in the early 1980s. SFBC emphasizes strengths and resilience of people by focusing on exceptions to their problems and their conceptualized solutions.

SFBC posits that it is not necessary to know the cause of a problem to solve it and there is no necessary relationship between the causes of the problems and their solutions. Any person might consider multiple solutions, and what is right for one person may not be right for others. In solution-focused counselling clients choose the goals they wish to accomplish, little attention is paid to diagnosis, history taking or exploring the emergence of the problem.

SFBC is grounded on the optimistic assumption that people are healthy and competent and have the ability to construct solutions that can enhance their lives. An underlying assumption of SFBC is that we already have the ability to resolve the challenges life brings us, but at times we lose our sense of direction or our awareness of our competence. Regardless of what shape clients are in when they enter, solution-focused counsellor believes clients are competent. The role of the counsellor is to help clients recognize the competencies they already possess and apply them towards solution. The essence of SFBC involves building on clients' hope and optimism by creating positive expectations that change is possible.

In addition to these alternative modes of counselling models represent postmodern approaches. One such model is **feminist model**. The feminist practitioners tend to employ consciousness raising techniques aimed at helping clients organize the impact of gender role socializations on their lives. The techniques include gender role analysis, power analysis, identifying and challenging untested beliefs, role playing and social action. Similarly, **family system counselling model** may be used. Techniques include genograms teaching, asking questions, joining the family, family mapping and setting boundaries. Since many parameters are changing across time and space, novel alternatives are expected in the future.

Chapter : 15

Self-Hypnosis

It is a common sense experience that administering therapies for psychological disorders and problems with adjustment is typically the domain of highly trained professionals. However, there are a few activities people can do safely on their own to reduce stress and change faulty habits.

It is advised that simple relaxation technique be used in self-hypnosis. Hypnosis does affect people differently, so some people will achieve greater relaxation using these techniques than will others. If you do not find more relaxed on your first attempt, more practice might be helpful.

In addition to bringing about a very relaxed state, self-hypnosis uses **affirmations,** or **positive suggestions,** related to your goals. For example, you might be feeling stressed about an upcoming job interview or exam. You can prepare a short list of affirmations prior to your self-hypnosis session that counts any doubts or negative thinking about your upcoming event. The best affirmations are specific, emotional and in the present tense: "I am very well-qualified for this job" or "I truly believe I have mastered the content of the course".

The next step is to put on some comfortable clothes and find a private, quiet place to sit down. Begin your session and relaxation. With each breath imagine waves of relaxation running from your head downward. Say to yourself, "I am feeling relaxed. With each breath I am becoming more relaxed". Some people prefer more traditional "I am feeling sleepy. My arms and legs are beginning to feel heavy". Once you are feeling completely relaxed, begin to attempt your affirmations with your relaxation statements. Some people prefer to record their affirmations and play them back during a session. Do this for 15 to 20 minutes or so, and see how you feel.

If your efforts are not providing the results you want, you might choose to invest in commercial recordings that are designed to help you achieve a relaxed state. You do not need to worry about being helplessly hypnotized in your home and unable to wake up.

Chapter : 16

Avoiding Overthinking

Overthinking is thinking too much, needlessly, passively, endlessly, and excessively pondering its meanings, causes and consequences of your character, your feelings, and your problems: "Why am I so unhappy? What will happen to me if I lose my job? What did he really mean when he made that remark on me?"

Many of us believe that when we face a problem, we should think deeply to find a solution. Yes! But too much analysis is paralysis. Numerous studies over the past two decades have shown that overthinking ushers in a host of adverse consequences. It sustains and worsens sadness, fosters negatively biased thinking, impairs a person's ability to solve problems, saps motivation, and interferes with concentration and initiative. Moreover, although people have a strong sense that they are gaining insight into themselves and their problems during their ruminations, this is rarely the case. What they gain is a distorted, pessimistic perspective on their lives.

The combination of rumination and negative mood is toxic. Research shows that people ruminate while sad are likely to feel powerless, self-critical, pessimistic, and generally negatively biased. The evidence that overthinking is bad for you is not vast. If you are someone plagued by ruminations, you are unlikely to become happier before you can break that habit. If you are an overthinker, one of the secrets to your happiness is the ability to allay obsessive overthinking, to reinterpret and redirect your negative thoughts into more neutral or optimistic ones. Happy people have the capacity to direct and absorb themselves in activities that divert their energies and attention away from anxious ruminations.

Daily life is replete with minor upsets, hassles, and reversals. In most people's experiences, other unavoidable events include illness, rejection, failure, and sometimes devastating trauma. However, those who react strongly to life's ups and downs, who have got difficulty shaking off unavoidable information are unhappy people.

Becoming happier means learning how to disengage from overthinking about both major and minor negative experiences, learning to stop searching for all the leaks and cracks --- at least for a time --- and not let them affect how you feel about yourself and your life as a whole.

Shaking Off Ruminations

Ruminations can be very compelling. You may combat overthinking and ruminations by adopting some effective strategies. Some of the strategies are listed below.

Cut loose. First, you need to free yourself from the clutch of your rumination. The first strategy to arrest overthinking is simple: **distract, distract, distract.** The distracting activity you select must be engrossing enough so that you don't have the opportunity to lapse back into ruminations. Good bets are activities that make you feel happy, curious, peaceful, amused, or proud. Read or watch something that's funny, listen to a song that's transporting, meet a friend for tea, do a physical activity that gets your heart rise up. It doesn't matter what you do, as long as it absorbs you, compels you, and isn't potentially harmful.

Although distraction seems like almost too simple, short-term solution or quick-fix, the positive emotions that it begets can "debias" your thinking (opening up a new, more objective, and more positive perspective on your troubles) and hone resources and skills (like creativity, sociability and problem-solving skills) that would be useful in future. Even a transient lift in mood can make you feel energetic.

The second strategy is the "**Stop**" **technique**, in which you think, say, or even shout to yourself: "Stop" or "No". Use your intellectual power to think about something else --- like your shopping list or what will you say when you call the man to repair your fridge. The technique is valuable in many situations, including moments when your thoughts wander even during a distracting pastime.

The third strategy directs us to set aside thirty minutes every day to do nothing but ruminating. Accordingly, if you find the negative thoughts pushing and pulling, you can truthfully tell yourself, "I can stop now, because I will have the opportunity to think about this later." Ideally, that thirty-minute period should be at a time of the day when you're not anxious or sad. More often than not, when the appointed time arrives, you will find it difficult and unnatural to force yourself to overthink.

The fourth strategy is to talk to a sympathetic and trusted person about your thoughts and problems. Choose carefully your sympathetic person. He or she must be able to think objectively, not make you feel even worse or end up ruminating out loud with you. You must not abuse this opportunity. If you bring your negative thoughts and worries ad infinitum, you may wear people out so much that they avoid you.

The final strategy involves writing. Whether in

a handsome journal, in a computer file, or on a scrap of paper, writing out your ruminations can help you organize them, make sense of them, and observe pattern that you haven't perceived before. Writing is also a way to unburden yourself of your negative thoughts --- to spill them on a page, so to speak --- allowing you to move past them.

Problem-solving action. You need to gain a new perspective on yourself and on your life in general. Essentially you need to try to solve the very real, concrete problems that might inspire your overthinking. For example, even if you're feeling weighed down by your problems and responsibilities and are indecisive about what to do, take a small step now. Perhaps this entails making an appointment with a doctor (even if you are pessimistic about doctor's expertise). If you're hesitant, think of a person whom you highly respect and admire and ask yourself which solution he or she would choose. Don't wait for something to happen or someone else to step in and help you Act right away. Even small steps will improve your mood and self-regard.

Avoiding future overthinking. You need to learn how to avoid future overthinking trips. For example, write a list of situations (places, persons, and time) that appear to trigger your overthinking. If at all possible, avoid those situations. This is not different from what a smoker must do when quitting, avoiding locations, time of the day and specific people that set off his desire to smoke.

If you are determined, learn how to meditate. The skill involved in this relaxation technique can help you distance yourself from your worries and ruminations and impart a positive sense of well-being.

Take in the big picture. In addition to the strategies discussed, one can combat overthinking with the help of a big picture. Will this matter in a year? Your answer will offer you a big picture view of your troubles and diminish your worries. If it remarkable how quickly things that seem so momentous and pressing this moment emerge as fairly trivial and insignificant. Sometimes when I am facing a horrendous week, I remind myself that I won't remember it one month, six months, or a year from now. (The more extreme version of this strategy is to use the deathbed criterion. Will it matter when you're on you deathbed?)

Another valuable approach is to distance yourself from rumination even further by contemplating your particular problem in the context of space and time. Visualize yourself (and the strains, worries, tribulations facing you) as a microscopic dot on earth, which is a tiny part of the Milky Way, which makes up an infinitesimal speck of the universe. This brings home the point that few things in life are so significant that they are worth overthinking.

Finally, if you resolve that the trouble you are enduring now is indeed significant and will matter in a year, then consider what experience it can teach you. Focusing on the lesson you can learn from a stress will help soften its blow. The lessons that these realities impart could be patience, perseverance, loyalty, or courage. Perhaps you are learning open-mindedness, forgiveness, generosity, or self-control.

Chapter : 17

Fighting Fear

B iopsychological research on emotion has focused to a large degree on fear and **defensive behaviour.** Fear is the emotional reaction to threat; it is the motivating force for defensive behaviours. Defensive behaviours are behaviours whose primary function is to protect the organism from threat or harm. In contrast, aggressive behaviours are behaviours whose primary function is to threaten or harm.

In the past decade, much of the research on the neural mechanism of emotion has focused on fear conditioning. **Fear conditioning** is the establishment of fear in response to a previously neutral stimulus (*the conditional stimulus*) by presenting it, usually several times, before the delivery of an aversive stimulus (*the unconditional* stimulus).

In the usual fear – conditioning experiment, the organism hears a tone (conditional stimulus) and then receives a mild electric shock to its feet (unconditional stimulus). After several pairing of the tone and the shock, the organism responds to the tone with a variety of defensive behaviours (e.g., freezing) and sympathetic nervous system responses (e.g., increased heart rate and blood pressure).

The search for the neural mechanism of fear conditioning has indicated that **amygdala** is involved in fear perception. Lesions of the amygdala blocks fear.

The amygdala receives input from all sensory systems, and it believed to be the structure in which the emotional significance of sensory signals is learned and retained.

In addition to amygdala, the **hippocampus** plays another important role. Environment, or *contexts*, in which fear-inducing stimuli are encountered can themselves come to elicit fear. For example, if we repeatedly encounter a bear on a particular trail in the forest, the trail itself would elicit fear in us. The process by which benign contexts come to elicit fear through their association with fear-inducing stimuli is called **Contextual fear conditioning.**

In view of the fact that the *hippocampus* plays a key role in memory, it is reasonable to expect that it would be involved in contextual fear conditioning.

Although fear has some adaptive functions, fear-induced thoughts and behaviours are largely stressful. Hence coping is required to regulate such negative emotions. A number of behavioural strategies have been suggested to fight fear.

Fighting Techniques

The famous essayist, Montaigne, once confessed: "The thing I fear most is fear". Fear casts its dark shadow over our lives at one time or another. Yet we can overcome it. The strategies can be adopted at cognitive, affective and behavioural levels.

Time out. It feels impossible to think clearly when we are flooded with fear. A racing heart, sweating palms and feeling panicky are the result of *adrenalin*. So, the first thing is to take time out so we can physically calm down. We may distract ourselves from the worry for 15 minutes by walking around the garden, making a cup of tea or having a both. When we have physically calmed down, we would feel better to decide on the best way to cope.

Exposure to fear. When we are anxious about something – be it work, a relationship or an exam – it can help to think through what the worst end result could be. Even if a presentation, a call or a conversation goes horribly wrong, chances are that we and the world will survive. Sometimes the worst can happen is a panic attack.

If we start to get a faster heartbeat or sweating palms, the best thing is not to fight it. We may stay where we are and simply feel the panic without trying to distract ourselves. Placing the palm of our hand on our stomach and breathing slowly and deeply (no more than 12 breaths a minute) helps soothe the body. It may take up to an hour, but eventually the panic will go away on its own. The goal is to help the mind get used to coping with panic, which takes the fear of fear away.

Avoiding fears only makes them scarier. If we panic one day getting into a lift, it's best to get back into a lift the next day. We may stand in the lift and feel the fear until it goes away.

Each time fears are embraced, it makes them easier to cope with the next time they strike, until in the end they are no longer a problem. We may try imagining the worst thing that can happen. Perhaps it's panicking and having a heart-attack. It's just not possible. The fear will run away.

Realistic thinking. Black-and-white perfectionist thinking such as "I'm a failure", or "my life is a mess", are unrealistic. Such unrealistic thinking brings the possibility of fear. Life is full of events; bad days and good days will always happen. It is not wise to remember only bad days. Sharing fears takes away a lot of scariness. We can talk to our friends, partners and advisers.

Visualization. It is helpful to close our eyes and imagine a place of safety and calm. It could be a picture of us walking on a beautiful beach or a happy memory from childhood.

Good treats. A good sleep, a wholesome meal or a walk are often the best cures for fear. Many people turn to alcohol or drugs to self-treat with the idea that it will make them feel better, but these only make nervousness worse. On the other hand, eating well will make us feel great physically and mentally.

Seeking support and connection. We should reach out to others who can provide support and comfort. If we need to talk about our feelings, we should choose a person who can listen and be with us as we struggle with fear. We need to stay away from people who minimize our feelings and tell us to "Get over it". Research shows social support is one of the most important predictive factors in fighting fear.

Self-compassion. We should treat ourselves and our feelings with tenderness and compassion. We need not push feelings away. We may seek a comforting environment in which to feel them. This may be with a friend or family member, while taking a bath, or while listening to soothing music. Meditation, with its dual focus on observing the breath and letting sensations come up, provides an excellent way of looking at feelings while remaining anchored in the present.

Journaling. We may write a narrative of how we found out about the event, the details that upset us, and our thoughts and feeling. Writing helps to recognize our reactions and make them more understandable.

Turning to the positive. It is wise to remind oneself that although the world contains much suffering and cruelty, it also contains much that is good. Deliberately we should think about the positive and uplifting things in our own lives and community. We need to think about the freedom and opportunity we have that many in the world have not.

Commitment to values. We need to think about our most important personal or spiritual values, including love for family, nonviolence, compassion, integrity, and so on. How does our current life reflect these values? We may make list of values and some concrete thing we can do in the next week or month to make them an even more important part of our lives. We may arrange a time to sit and talk about our family's most important values. Making a poster, list, or vision board reflecting core values are very useful.

Feeling grateful. We may feel gratitude when we focus on the people in our lives, past and present that have provided us with protection, nurturance, and love. We can bring to mind an image of ourselves with that person. We may focus on how we feel in that person's presence. Then we may think about the gratitude we feel for what that person has given us. We may find some concrete ways to express that gratitude, through demonstration of affection, a letter, a gift, or just telling them we appreciate them.

Doing something constructive. It is effective to channel our fear into constructive activities to help improve the situation. This may include sending letters of support to the disadvantaged volunteering at service centres, writing letters to the editors of local papers, or lobbying politicians for the needed changes on a societal level. Taking actions can combat feelings helplessness or guilt and can contribute to increasing safety or goodness in the world.

Chapter : 18

Anger Management

Anger is a normal human emotion and when it is managed properly it is not a problem. Everyone gets angry, and mild anger can sometimes be useful to deal with situations. In the sense it has adaptive functions. However, if anger is expressed in harmful ways, or if persists over a long period of time, then it can lead to problems of relationship at home and at work and can affect the overall quality of our lives.

It is "an emotional state that varies in intensity from mild irritation to intense fury and rage", according to Charles Spielberger, a psychologist known for his work on anger. Like other emotions it is accompanied by biological changes. When we get angry our heart rate and blood pressure go up, as do as levels of our energy hormones, adrenaline, and nonadrenaline.

Anger is often associated with frustration – things don't always happen the way we want and people don't always behave the way we think they should. Anger is usually linked with other negative emotions or is a response to them. We may be feeling hurt, frightened, disappointed, worried, embarrassed or frustrated, but may express these sorts of feelings as anger. Anger can also result from misunderstandings or poor communication between people.

Men and women often, but not always manage and express anger.

The instinctive, natural way to express anger is to respond aggressively. Anger is a natural adaptive response to threats. It prompts powerful, often aggressive feelings and behaviours, which allow us to fight and defend ourselves when we are attached.

On the other hand, we can't physically lash out at every person or object that irritates or annoys us. People use a variety of both conscious and unconscious processes to deal with their angry feelings. The three main approaches are *expressing*, suppressing, and *calming*. Expressing our angry feelings is an assertive – not aggressive – manner is the healthiest way to express anger. To do this, we have to learn how to make clear what are needs are, and how to get them met, without hurting others. Being assertive does not mean being pushy or demanding it means being respectful of ourselves and others.

Men and women often, but not always, manage and express anger in different ways. With men, anger may be the primary emotion, as many men believe that anger is a more legitimate emotion to express in a situation. Often men find it harder to express the feelings underneath the anger, like hurt, sadness or grief. For women the reverse may often be true – the anger get buried under tears.

Anger becomes a problem when it creates trouble for us with other people, our work, our health, day-to-day living or the law. It is a problem when other people around us are frightened, hurt or feel that they cannot talk to us or disagree with us in case we become angry. Some indicators of problem are listed below

- Anger involves verbal, emotional, physical or psychological abuse.

- We feel angry a lot of time
- It is leading to problems with personal relationship and work.
- We think we have to get angry to get what we want
- It lasts for a long time
- It affects other situations not related to the original event
- We become anxious or depressed about our anger
- We use alcohol or other drugs to try to manage our anger.

Management Strategies

Anger can be suppressed and then converted or redirected. This happens when we hold in our anger, stop thinking about it, and focus on something positive. The aim is to inhibit or suppress our anger and convert it into more constructive behavior. The danger in this type of response is that if it is not allowed outward expression, our anger can turn inward. Anger turned inward may cause hypertension, high blood pressure, or depression.

Unexpressed anger can create other problems. It can lead to pathological expressions of anger, such as passive-aggressive behaviour (getting back at people indirectly, without telling them why, rather than confronting them head-on) or a personality that seems perpetually cynical and hostile. People who are constantly putting others down, criticizing everything, and making cynical comments haven't learned how to constructively express their anger. Not surprisingly, they aren't likely to have many successful relationships. Finally, we can calm down inside. This means not just controlling our outward behaviour, but also controlling our internal responses, taking steps to lower our heart rate, calm ourselves down, and let the feelings subside.

Some people used to believe that venting anger is beneficial. Researchers have now found that "letting it up" actually escalates anger and aggression and does nothing to resolve the situation.

The goal of anger management is to reduce both our emotional feelings and the physiological arousal that anger causes. *We can't get rid of, or avoid, the things or the people that enrage us, nor can we change them, we can learn to control our reactions.* Here are some strategies to keep anger at bay.

Relaxation. Simple relaxation techniques such as deep breathing and relaxing imagery can help calm down angry feelings. There are books and brochures that teach us relaxation techniques. We can try some simple steps:

- Breathing deeply from our diaphragm, breathing from chest won't relax us. It is helpful to picture our breath coming from our "gut".
- It is useful to slowly repeat a calm word or phrase such as "relax", take it easy". We should repeat it to ourselves while breathing deeply.
- We may use imagery, visualizing a relaxing experiencing, from either our memory or our imagination.
- Nonstrenuous, slow yoga-like exercises can help our muscles and make us feel much calmer
- We should practice these techniques daily. We would learn

Cognitive restructuring. Anger management requires cognitive restructuring. This means changing the way we think. Angry people tend to curse, swear or speak in highly colourful terms that reflect their inner thoughts. When we are angry, our thinking can get very exaggerated and overly dramatic. We may replace these thoughts with non-rational ones. For instance, instead of telling ourselves, "oh, it's awful, it's terrible, everything is ruined, we may tell ourselves," it's frustrating, and it's understandable that I'm upset about it, but it's not the end of the world and getting angry is not going to fix it anyhow". We may avoid the words like "never" or "always" when talking about ourselves or someone else. "This would never work", or "you are always forgetful" – these expressions would be harmful.

We should remind ourselves getting angry is not going to fix anything. We should also remind ourselves that the "world is not to get us," "we are just experiencing some of the rough spots of daily life". In other words, saying, "I would like" something is healthier than saying, "I demand" or "I must have something."

Problem solving. Sometimes our anger and frustration are caused by very real and inescapable problems in our lives. Yet every problem has a solution. We may recognize the problem, make a plan for its resolution and check our progress along the way. It is better to adopt proactive coping. If not possible, confrontative strategy would be fine. It is not appropriate to evade the problem.

Better communication. Angry people jump to the conclusions very fast. Yet conclusions can be very inaccurate. It is wise to slow down and think through our responses. We need not say the first thing that comes into our head, but slow down and think carefully about what we want to say. At the same time, we must listen carefully to what the other person is saying.

*Using humour.*Humour can help defuse rage in a number of ways. When we get angry and call someone a name or refer to them in some imaginative phrase, we may stop and picture what that word would literally look like. If we feel like calling our colleagues "dirtbag", imagining a large bag full of dirt would defuse our anger.

Changing our environment. It is possible that some aspects of our immediate environment are causing irritation. If we know that some aspects are particularly stressful, we may change that negative portion.

In addition to these strategies, a few other tips are very helpful.

Helpful Tips

- **List things that can trigger your anger.**

  Make a list of the things that often set off your anger (for example, your teenager leaving dirty dishes in the sink). If you know ahead of time, you may be able to avoid these things or do something different when they happen

- **Notice the warning signs of anger in your body.**

  Notice things that happen to your body (for example, heart pounding). The earlier you recognize, the more successful you will be at calming yourself.

- **Use self-talks.**

  Develop a list of things you may say to yourself before, during and after anger-provoking situations.

  Before:

  "I will be able to handle this". "If I get angry, I know what to do".

  During:

  "Stay calm, relax, and breathe easy". "Stay calm, I'm ok".

  After:

  "I managed that well. I can do". "I felt angry, but I didn't lose my cool."

- **Take time out.**

  If you feel your anger getting out of control, take time out from a situation or an argument. Try stepping out of the room, or going for a walk. Before you go, remember to make a time to talk about the situation later when everyone involved has calmed down. During a time out, plan how you are going to stay calm when your conversation resumes.

- **Use distraction.**
  A familiar strategy for managing anger is to distract your mind from the anger-provoking situation. Try counting to twenty, playing soothing music, talking to a good firend, or focusing on a simple task like ironing dresses.
- **Try to acknowledge what is making you angry.**
  Acknowledge things that make you angry. Sometimes it can help you to write things down. What is happening in your life? How do you feel about the things that are happening? If some close friends can give advice, seek it. Work out some options for changing your option.
- **Rehearse anger management skills.**
  Use your imagination to practice your anger management strategies.
- **Smile, smile, all the while.**
  "You are not completely dressed if you do not wear a smile"

  Mahatma Gandhi

Chapter : 19

Managing Self-Control

In a new book, psychologist Walter Mischel discussed how we can all become better at resisting temptations, and why doing so can improve our lives.

Mischel was first drawn to studying this problem when his children were very young. He was a young faculty member at Stanford, and his three daughters were very closely spaced in age, between 2 and 5 years old. Mischel had an interesting observation. Mischel found that one of his daughters was very intolerant; she would be nagging her mother if there is slight delay in serving the desert following the dinner.

This drew him to the question of how self-control is mastered, how it develops naturally, and what we can do to increase it in our children or ourselves. What are the mental and – years later – what are the brain mechanisms that make emotional self-regulation and behavioural self-regulation possible?

Mischel went to an elementary school and conducted an interesting study. He asked whether they would like to have one marshmallows that day or two marshmallows the next day (it is comparable to having one *rasogullah* today versus two rasogullahs tomorrow, in Indian conditions).

Obviously a lot of children preferred one marshmallow, only a small number of children chose to wait for the next day's reward. The **delay of gratification** exhibited by a small number of children surprise Mischel. In order to probe into the matter, Mischel asked these children about the secret of their control. Most of them replied that they used *self-talk* and *visualization*. They kept on saying to themselves: "Hey! Just wait you would get two marshmallow tomorrow. You would enjoy eating the two while your friends would not be having anything tomorrow". These children also used visualization. They constructed mental imaging of eating marshmallow the next day while others would be wandering away. These children who as 4-year-olds, could resist a tempting marshmallow placed in front of them, and instead hold out for a larger reward in the future (two marshmallows).

The Marshmallow Test did not stop there. Mischel identified these children who demonstrated commendable level of delay of gratification. He followed them up for about half a century and the resulting outcome is a scientific achievement on to part of Walter Mischel and social benefits for parents, teachers, educator, and community at large. The book that contains these lessons and is recently published is titled "**The Marshmallow Test**".

The preschoolers who showed delay of gratification become adults who were more likely to finish college and earn higher incomes. They were less likely to become vulnerable for overweight, addiction and misadventure.

Mischel argues that the strategies the successful preschooler used can be taught to people of all ages. We can use self-talk; we can employ visualization. We can all improve our ability to achieve our goals.

The good news that this cognitive and emotional skill set is eminently teachable, particularly early in life. It is great in preschool; it's great within the first few years of life. It's great in adolescence even. And it continues to be a skill set that can be developed when we are quite mature adults.

Mischel further maintains that children can be taught in many interesting and child-friendly ways. A particular good example of that are studies Michael Posner and his colleagues at the University of Oregon (USA) are doing. They worked with 4- to 6-year-old kids, and the idea was to help them acquire better self-control using a computer game. For example, in one of the exercises, there is a cat in a rainstorm. The children's job is to use a joystick that controls an umbrella to keep the cat dry as it runs around. So this is teaching control functions: I have a goal, I have to keep the umbrella over the cat's head. I can't be distracted and start looking around. I have to keep the umbrella over the cat's head.

Posner and his colleagues found that five sessions of 40 minutes each with these kids led to substantial increases in their control functions.

It is really the story of resistance to temptation – the story of Adam and Eve in the Garden of Eden – that Mischel was interested in and that's how the marshmallow test was born. He is still following the original participants from the Stanford marshmallow study. They are now between their very late forties and early fifties. A sample of about 110 of the original Stanford children is there. The researcher is interested to examine the relationship between maintaining these two different patterns of high self-control over the life course versus low self-control over the life course.

As indicated earlier, positive outcomes (greater school and college achievement, social adaptation, stress-free life and job success) have been demonstrated.

How do parents develop these skills in their children?

- If you want your children to have self-control, you need to model it: you can't expect kids to develop to delay gratification if you are breaking your promises to them.
- Kids also need to learn that their behavior has consequences. If they behave in constructive and creative ways, the consequences are good. If they behave in destructive ways, the consequences are not so good.
- Teach children to use "self-talk" and to construct positive visual imageries.

Chapter : 20

Planning

Developing clear and specific implementation intentions seem to enhance goal accomplishment. In a study, university students were asked to describe a difficult and an easy project they intended to complete. Projects include such things as writing a class report working on resolving a family conflict, and participating in an athletic competition. Students were asked to if they had specific plans about when, when, and how to get started on each project. Project completion was checked after submission deadline was over.

For difficult problems, implementation intentions was clearly related to successful completion. Two thirds of students who had made implementation intentions finished their projects. Only one-fourth of the students who had not made plans finished their projects. In other words, without specific plans for implementing their goals, most students failed to achieve this. For easier projects, implementation plans were unrelated to completion. Whether they had made plans or not, 80% of the students finished their easy projects.

In another study students were asked to prepare a report. They were asked to describe as to how they would celebrate an important festival. Students were instructed to write their reports not later than 48 hours before the festival and send the report to the experimenter. Half of the students in this study were asked to form implementation plan by describing exactly when and where they would write the report. The other half were not instructed to make implementation plan. The value of thinking ahead was again shown, with 75% of students who made plans returned their reports within deadline. In contrast, only 33% of the non implementation group completed their reports on time.

Implementation plan helps in a big was. It creates mental and environmental markers that make self-regulation more efficient, more automatic, and less susceptible to distractions and preoccupation. Most of us lead busy lives. We have multiple goals we want to achieve. Without imposing some structure on lives we can easily caught up on the bustle of daily events. Connecting personal goals to specific plans concerning how, when, and where we will work on them makes our goals easier to remember by specifying a time and place for a goal activity, we create environmental cues that may lead to a relatively automatic activation of goal-directed behaviour. For example, consider a student who decides to study mathematics every alternate morning (7 am to 9 am). Over time, the behaviour may not require much conscious effort or self-control to activate. That is, studying mathematics at a specific time and place may become a routine, like taking a bath every morning. Few of us make plans for taking baths. We just automatically do it because it is a part of our daily ritual. It is believed that implementation intentions contribute to effective self-regulation by passing the control of one's behaviour to the environment and thereby bypassing some of the distractions that affect more conscious effortful self-control.

These conclusions are supported by studies of automaticity in behaviour control. With enough repetition and consistent pairing of internal and external events, many behaviours can "run off" with little or no conscious control. Driving a car serves as an example. A beginning driver has to pay close, conscious attention to steering, signaling, monitoring surrounding traffic, braking and checking mirrors. Experience drivers do all these things automatically. Our ability to listen to the radio or converse with fellow passengers while driving are possible because the adjustments necessary to respond to changes in the speed of the car be made without requiring conscious controlled action. The value of such "automatic guidance system" is that they efficiently and effectively control behaviour without imposing a penalty on energy expenditure. In contrast conscious self-control comes with an energy price tag.

Chapter : 21

Strengthening Work-Life Balance

Millennials of both gender are more interested in the quality of their work-life compared to their counterparts in the past. How can early career professionals handle this new life phase with more grace and less stress? Here is some advice from psychological research and early career navigators who have been successful.

1. **Map put your work life:** For early career professionals, the importance of good career planning cannot be overestimated. You need to do extra–planning to accommodate your expanded responsibilities and family time. You need to discuss with senior colleagues to know where responsibilities are heaviest and where they are lightest. Then mentally make yourself a spreadsheet of what the year will look like. This type of **forethought** is essential if you are planning to move forward and maintain a balance. Such forethought should include educating yourself about your employer's leave policies, creating a career plan that accommodates work and family, even your work priorities. This legwork is especially important for working women with children are much more likely to face the challenge.

2. **Plan at home too.** Specifically mapping out the ingredients of family life can waylay potential conflicts and promise more harmony at home. When women do

more household chores than men – particularly when they believe the work should be divided equally – they are less happy than women who share duties equally. The decision to divide child care and family activities in ways that match their schedules and energies is very helpful. For example, the lady of the house taking the morning shift can get the kids up and dressed and off to school. Her husband may manage after the school by picking up the kids, helping them with homework, and getting dinner started.

3. **Use your training.** With a view to attaining work-life balance, the restructuring of thought is needed at times. For example, one of the partners holds a steady job and earns a lot of money. Another is self-employed. The lack of parity in money making may bring some conflicts. Yet the self-employed partner may reframe his/her self-employment as an opportunity for a flexible autonomous lifestyle versus a stressful grind.

   "Instead of thinking about how much money I am not making, I try to think about how fortunate I am to be able to make time off when I need to," the self-employed person says. This view helps him/her appreciate his/her ability to take vacations and attend children's school concert and sporting events with less anxiety.

4. **Be a better communicator.** It is important that members of a family must work as a team. Being direct about their preferences and ideas is a key factor. **Partner communication** includes communicating practical needs. The willingness to give help and seek help is a positive attitude to give feedback and receive feedback improves the quality of communication.

5. **Know your boundaries.** Many early career professionals need to learn the art of letting go of activities that are

bogging down work or family. For examples, a woman used to see patients till late evening. But she is now blessed with a child and child care demands her time and energy. In such a changed scenario, she may decide to stop seeing patients late in the evening and to forgo chairing a volunteer committee. At one point, she may choose to regularly leave work at 4 p.m., so she could get home early enough to enjoy her kids before bed.

6. **Eschew perfectionism.** It may be necessary to eschew perfectionism, at least temporarily. While relinquishing the urge to do everything at his/her highest level, it helps to keep balance.

7. **Take care of yourself.** It may be hard to fit exercise and other forms of self-care into your routine when you are responsible for two large completing worlds. But self-care can foster work-life balance. Researchers indicate that employees who report healthy eating, regular exercise and sound sleep were more likely to have high job performance.

8. **Ask for and offer help.** In the context of work-family balance, the connectivity and reciprocity is essential. There are many situations where our neighbours and friends come to our rescue at the time of need. The bond is strengthened when we offer help to others and also seek help from others.

9. **Play it forward.** Finally, good balance means thinking those who have helped to find it. When you think of people who have mentored you and who continue to mentor you, you feel rewarding to give back to others in the same way. Together we can work to figure out what we need to do to help them the best.

Chapter : 22

Managing Oneself

We live in an age of unprecedented opportunity. One can rise to the top of one's chosen profession, regardless of where one starts out. It is possible to carve out one's place, to know when to change course, and to keep oneself engaged and productive during work life that they span some 50 years. To do these things well, one needs to cultivate a deep understanding of oneself – not only what one's strengths and weaknesses are but also how one learns, how one works with others, what one's values are, and where one can make the greatest contribution. Because only when one operates from strengths can one achieve true excellence.

Many people think they know who they are good at. They are usually wrong. More often, people know what they are good at – and even then more people are wrong than right.

The only way to discover our strength is through *feedback analysis*. Whenever we make a key decision or take a key action, it is useful to write down what we expect will happen. Nine or twelve months later we could compare the actual results with our expectations.

Practiced consistently, this simple method will show

us within a fairly short period of time, may be two or three years, where our strengths lie – and this the best important things to know. This method will show us what we are doing or failing to do that deprives us of the full benefits of our strengths; it will show us where we are particularly competent. It will also show us where we have no strengths and cannot perform.

Several implications for action follow feedback analysis. First and foremost is the concentration on one's strength. Second, analysis will rapidly show where one needs to improve skill or acquire new ones. It will also show gaps in our knowledge – and those can usually be filled. Third, it is possible to discover where our intellectual arrogance is causing disabling ignorance for too many people.

It is essentially to remedy our bad habits – the things we do or fail to do that inhibit our effectiveness and performance. Such habits will quickly show up in the feedback. At the same time, feedback will also reveal when the problem is a lack of manners. Manners – simple things like say "please" and "thank you" and knowing a person's name – enable two people to work together whether they like each other or not.

Performing Style

Amazingly few people know how they get things done. Indeed, most of us do not even know that *people work and perform differently.* Too many people work in ways that are not their ways and that almost guarantees nonperformance.

Like one's strength, how one performs is unique. It is a matter of personality. Whether personality is a matter of nature or nurture, it surely is formed long before a person goes to work. And *how* a person performs is a given, just as *what* a person is good at or not good at is a given. A person's way of performing can be slightly modified, but it is unlikely to be completely changed – and certainly not easily. Just as people achieve results by doing what they are good at, they also achieve results by working in ways that they best perform.

Writers do not, as a whole, learn by listening and reading. They learn by writing. Because schools do not allow them to learn this way, they get poor grades. RabindraNath Tagore and Winston Churchill are classic examples.

There are people who learn by writing. Same people learn by taking copious notes. Beethoven, for example, left behind an enormous number of sketchbooks, yet he said he never actually looked at them when he composed. Asked why he kept them, he is reported to have replied, "If I don't write it down immediately, I forget it right way. If I put it into a sketchbook, I never forget it and I never have to look at it up again".

Some people learn by doing. Others learn by hearing them talk. Learning through talking is by no means an unusual method. Successful trial lawyers learn the same way as do many medical diagnosticians.

Of all the important pieces of self-knowledge, understanding how we learn is the easiest to acquire.

Some people work best as subordinates. General George Patton, the great American military hero of World War II, is a prime example. Yet when he was proposed for an independent command, General George Marshall the US Chief of Staff and probably the most successful picker of men in U.S. history – said, "Patton is the best subordinate the American army has ever produced, but he would be the worst commander".

Some people work best as team members. Others work best alone. Some are exceptionally talented as coaches and mentors; others are simply incompetent as mentors. A great many people perform best as advisors but cannot take the burden and pressure of taking decisions. A good many other people, by contrast, need an advisor to force themselves to think, then they can make decisions and act on them with speed, self-confidence and courage.

Other important question to ask include: Do I perform well under stress, do I need a highly structured and predictable environment? Do I work in a big organization or a small one?

A search for these answers would enhance self-understanding. We need not try to change ourselves – we are unlikely to succeed. It is better to work hard to improve the way we perform.

Mirror Test

In order to manage ourselves, we need to ask: what are our values? This is not a question of ethics. With respect to ethics, the rules are the same for everybody. But ethics is only part of a value system – especially of an organization's value system.

To work in an system whose values system is unacceptable or incompatible with one's won condemns a person both to frustration and to nonperformance. Whether a pharmaceutical company tries to obtain results by making constant, small improvement or by achieving occasional, highly expensive, and risky "breakthroughs" is not primarily an economic question. The result of either strategy may be pretty much the same. At bottom, there is a conflict in value system.

Knowing One's Place

A small number of people know very easily where they belong. Mathematicians, musicians, and cooks, for instance, are usually mathematicians, musicians, and cooks by the time they are four or five years old. Physicians usually develop on their career in their teens, if not earlier. But most people, usually gifted people, do not easily know where they belong until they are well past their mid-twenties. By that time, however, they should know the answers to these questions: what are my strengths? How do I perform? What are my values?

Successful careers are not planned. They develop when people are prepared for opportunities because they know their strengths, their method of work and their values. Knowing where one belong can transform an ordinary person – hardworking and competent but otherwise mediocre – into an outstanding performer.

Throughout history, the great majority of people never had to ask the question: What should I contribute? They were told to what to contribute, and their tasks were dictated rather by the work itself – as it was for a peasant or artisan – or by a master. And until very recently, it was taken for granted that most people were subordinates who did as they were told. Even in the 1950's and 1960's, the new knowledge workers looked to their company's personnel department to plan their careers.

Then in the late 1960's, no one wanted to be told what to do any longer. Young men and women began to ask what do I want do? And what they heard was that the way to contribute was to "do your own thing". But this solution was as wrong as the previous. Very few of the people believed that doing one's own thing would lead to contribution, self-fulfillness and success achieved any of the three.

Knowledge workers have to learn to ask a question that has not been asked in the past, what *should* my contribution be? To answer this, they must address, three different elements. What does the situation require? Given my strengths, my way of performing, and my values, how can I make the greatest contribution to what needs to be done? And finally, what results here to be achieved to make a difference.

It is rarely possible to look too for ahead. A plan can usually cover no more than 18 months and still be reasonably clear and specific. So the question in most cases should be, where and how can I achieve results that will make a difference within the next year and a half. The result should be hard to achieve, they should require "stretching" to use the current buzzword. But they should be within reach. In addition, results should be visible and measurable.

Responsibility for Relationship

Very few people work by themselves and achieve results by themselves – a few great artists, a few great scientists, a few great athletes. Most people work with others and are effective with other people. This is true whether they are members of an organization or independently self-employed. Managing oneself requires taking responsibility for relation. This has two parts.

The first is to accept the fact the other people are as much individuals as we ourselves are. They have their strengths and weaknesses. To be effective, one has to know their strengths, values, and performance styles.

The second part of relationship responsibility is taking responsibility for communication. Personality conflict is a common problem in organization. In fact, knowledge workers should communicate with every one with whom they work, colleague, or team member. People should know others' strengths, their values, their performing styles and expected contribution. Thus, the first secret of effectiveness is to understand the people one works with so that one can make use of their strengths.

Chapter : 23

Management of Pain

Pain and injury are inevitable consequences of our day-to-day lives. People participating in athletics experience it more often; muscle pain and back aches happen to be routine matters for them. The extent of pain experienced depends on a number of factors. The context in which injury occurs, our emotional state at the time, the way we interpret the injury, and the expectations of the culture contribute to the perception of pain. Although we should do everything to avoid injury, there are several things that be done to lessen the impact of pain.

With a view to dealing with pain, we may use counterirritants to relieve the pain. There is an interesting concept called the **gate-control theory** of pain. It posits the existence of gates, neural mechanisms in the spinal cord that sometimes close, thereby preventing pain messages from reaching the brain. The use of counterirritants, which stimulate or irritate a nearby area, and close the pain gate and thereby reduce pain. Deep massages, ice packs or heat applied to the injured area can be effective in relieving muscle pain people experience. People who experience chronic forms of pain find relief through other counterirritant techniques. Acupuncture is a pain-relief technique in which needles are inserted into various locations on the body. Stimulating specific points on the fingers seem to reduce dental and facial pain.

Similarly, electrical stimulation applied through devices implanted on the brain or spinal cord may be helpful. Stimulation applied on the surface of the skin (transcutaneous electrical nerve stimulation or TENS) is found to be effective for back pain.

Another effective technique used for pain management involves **cognitive behavioural method.** This technique changes the way we think about pain. Research shows that dwelling on negative thoughts usually intensifies our perception of pain. In contrast, substituting positive thoughts for negative ones can be an effective countermeasure. **Distraction** can alleviate pain, by shifting the focus on attention away from the pain. A good way to accomplish this is to select enjoyable activities that fully engage our attention, such as a good movie or activities with friends. Another technique to get our mind off the pain is to induce an emotional state incompatible with pain, such as **laughter**. We can expose ourselves as quickly as possible to something - or someone – we find humorous. The pain we are experiencing may quickly abate.

While techniques are available to deal with pain, pain signals should not be completely ignored. Pain serves as a signal for greater problem. On the basis of this warning, we should take steps for durable solutions, long-term solutions. We should consult specialists and experts if pain persists. A healthy approach to life involves both the immediate management of pain and duration remediation in the direction.

Chapter : 24

Strengthening Spiritual Practice

Aspiritual worldview gives you the feeling that life has meaning. The word *spiritual* is used to mean many different things. Many persons immediately think of organized religion when the word *spiritual* is mentioned. Indeed, most people pursue their spiritual development through religion. Others, however, pursue their spiritual development outside of formal, institutionalized religion. Whether inside or outside of formal religion, spirituality gives you the feeling of being connected to something that is larger and more important than your narrow sense of ego.

The "Something" may be thought of as a supreme being, the life force, creative evolution, or a cause such as world peace, God, the Ultimate, the Tao, Krishna, Brahma, Allah, Buddha, or the Jesus – many names are used to refer to the "Something". In every case, they refer to the ultimate good in the universe. In some traditions the "Something" is thought of as being largely transcendent. In other tradition it is said to be immanent (dwelling within us).

Herbert Benson, Harvard cardiologist, developed a measure of spirituality. The scale measures the feeling that *there is more than just me.* The feeling is not necessarily religious in the traditional sense but it is related to greater mental health.

Increased Self-Awareness

Spiritual practice leads to increased self-awareness. Self-awareness does not mean self-consciousness. Self-consciousness is fearful preoccupation with oneself stemming from a lack of self-respect and self-confidence. When self-conscious people face challenging situations, they feel threatened and their attention turns inward damage control.

Self-awareness, on the other hand, is a matter of recognizing what you are doing and why you are doing it *while* you are doing it. This awareness brings freedom. Self-awareness brings self-respect and self-confidence.

Expanded Self-Identity

Spiritual practice also leads to an expanded self-identity. The sense of connectedness with a force larger than yourself frees you from ego encapsulation. Energy is freed up from the defense of the ego and made available for higher pursuits. Spiritual practice move you from a narrow preoccupation with your ego interest to a greater concern for the welfare of others.

Practice Stages

For the sake of practice, stage-wise progress can be charted. Stage 1 is a stage of undisciplined spirituality. People stuck at this stage are governed purely by own interest without respect to the interests of others. During Stage 2, the person rigidly conforms to formal, institutionalized religious prescriptions. There is a blind allegiance to the letter of the prescription. At the Stage 3, people feel free to interpret religious teachings and practices according to their understanding. They are not intent on destroying the faith of others. They trust their own intelligence and motivation enough to reinterpret religious prescriptions based on their own experiences.

During the final stage (Stage 4), people have moved beyond the narrowness of their religious tradition and embrace other persons coming out of other religious tradition as well. They understand that religious traditions represent the cumulative wisdom of a people at a given print of time, and these traditions with their rituals are merely fingers printing to the Ultimate. They understand that the Ultimate, the Force, God cannot be fully comprehended. Lao Tsu writes: "The Tao that can be named is not the eternal Tao. The name that can be named is not the eternal name". People who reach stage four are willing to accept the mystery and to honour others interpretation.

Spirituality thus, creates a rich interior life – the development of interests that transcend the busyness of our lives. Mindless busyness interferes with the development of spirituality.

Points to Ponder
1. Spirituality is not a product, it is a process – a process of developing healthy approach.
2. Grow through the stages indicated and create a rich interior of life.

Chapter : 25

The Secret of Living Together

*L*iving together happily is both a challenge and an opportunity. *Because of many difficulties and problems, the prospect of living together has been clouded. The points that follow would guide us to live together happily. It is expected that our readers would derive great benefits out of this write-up.*

Marriage and well-being are strongly connected. A successful marriage is one of the most powerful contributors to enriched individual health and happiness. Unhappy marriages have an equally strong connection to unhappiness and diminished health. Since most people marry, the level of well-being within a society as whole would depend on the quality of happy marriages.

Statistics regarding the status of marriage do not present a rosy picture. Major reviews of census data in the West do present pessimistic scenarios. In the United States, some 50% of all new marriages end in divorce or separation. Other western countries, such as the Netherlands, Sweden, Canada, and England, have also witnessed increases in divorce, but US divorce rates are nearly double those of other developed countries. Divorce rates have always been higher within the first 5 to 7 years of marriages, consistent with the conventional wisdom about the '7-year-itch'.

However, today many longer-term marriages also fail (i.e., 10 years and up). These appears to be no 'safe' point beyond which all marriages last, although after 15 years, the divorce rate drops substantially.

The percentage of people who live together before marriage has increased dramatically. Nearly a third of American households are made of unmarried men and women living together. An estimated 50% of college students live with a romantic partner without getting married. Does cohabitation increase the success of a future marriage? The idea that a 'trial marriage' may help partners to know them well is undercut by the fact that these cohabiting couples have higher divorce rate than non-cohabiting couples. It appears that the lack of strength of commitment on the part of co habiting partners is a possible causal factor.

Although divorce rates in India is not very disturbing, we have to attend to warning signal. The divorce rate is still lower compared to world scenarios. Out of 1,000 marriages in India, 11 marriages terminate in a divorce. These statistics were lower in 1990, when out of 1000 marriages just 7.4 percent marriages ended up in a divorce. The divorce rate is higher in urban areas compared to rural setting. In the 21st century rates in the cities have been shooting up alarmingly. In Delhi, rates doubled in five years. In Bangalore, rates tripled in four years. These are very shocking statistics.

In the Indian context, research has identified a number of causal factors. These include work pressure and stress, economical security, haphazard working hours, lack of time to spend in the house with family and financial freedom. The Chairperson of Women's Commission has disclosed that in a majority of cases, the marital discord has stemmed from an unsatisfactory physical relationship.

The Chairperson's opinion is that as the people are viewing the computer screen for prolonged periods, this has led to impotency. Some psychiatrists have pointed out the role of job stress in marital discord.

It is axiomatic that increased freedom and decreased constraints have played significant roles in the rate of enhanced failures of marriages. In the past, unhappy married couples had to face a number of constraints. First, women did not enjoy much economic freedom and they had to depend on their husbands for day-to-day living. Second, divorce at one time carried a significant cultural stigma for both men and women. Third, the importance of staying together for the sake of children was a strong consideration. Fourth, a belief about the sanctity of marriage was strong. Furthermore, the courts and legal system have greatly reduced the difficulties of divorce and separation.

Uniqueness of Lasting Marriages

Instead of explaining the causes of failed marriages, it is more appropriate to examine factors of uniqueness of lasting marriages. Today, choice and love are playing increasing roles in mate selection. We can think about a question: If a person had all the other qualities one desires, would one marry the person if one is not in love? When American college students were surveyed in 1967, 45% of men and 76% of women said yes to this question. Men evidently had more romantic attitude whereas women were practical. However, four decades later, no was the overwhelming answer to the same question by both men and women. The prominence of love to prevail over differences in social status, religion, background and life events is a regular theme in movies and television programmes.

Large scale surveys indicate the importance of loving and liking in selection of marriage partners. Buss asked over 10,000 people from 37 countries to rate 18 characteristics according to their desirability in mate selection. Despite cultural differences the number one criterion for mate selection was love or mutual attraction.

Despite such positive human bonding, the increasing rate of failures of marriage prompts us to look happy couples. What are the forces that cement the relationship permanently? Psychologists have empirically delineated a number of interesting features of successful marriages.

1. Be a mother as well as a Mentor

Blend of Realism and Idealism. The value of a good mix of realism and idealization is supported by research. It is found that some degree of idealization contributes to couple's happiness and satisfaction. Couples who have the most positive view of each other's personal attributes are not only happier, but they are less likely to break up. The tendency to view our partners more positively than they see themselves means that we overlook our partners' shortcoming. This is the view that mothers have of their children. They see the best in their kids and downplay faults. The mutuality of this idealization enhances self-esteem and satisfaction.

People desire evaluations than affirm or verify their own self-views. More specifically, people want positive feedback about their positive qualities. We each want verification of our won self-views. Relationships are enhanced when your partner affirms your own self-view because this proves that she or he knows you as you know yourself. The authencity of your partner's understanding of "who you really are" creates strong feeling of intimacy.

The opposing nature of idealization is also needed. Idealization is essential in short-term relationship and at the beginning of marriage. As relationship matures more accurate information becomes important. Two much idealization may do harm for a long-term relationship. If one of the partner is involved in drinking or gambling, it would be improper for the other to remain silent. An accurate understanding of partner's shortcoming and its expression would be needed for the furtherance of long-term relationship. In short, both idealization and reality are to be blended in their combination of differential proportion during the developing course of relationship.

2. Develop Friendly Attitude

Friendship Mindset. The second powerful determinant of happy married relation is the mind-set reflected in the context of best friendship. The impact of strong commitment is evinced in these cases. With passage of time, passion declines. Yet intimacy and commitment grow. They may stay home by themselves, perhaps each engrossed in a book, as long as they are across each other. Such married couples exhibit attitudes, values and behaviours that are found in two persons who are tied by the thread of best friendship.

3. Foster Secure Attachment Style

Attachment Styles. It is a common experience that our primary bonding with our mothers offers us a resource of great significance. For the first-time, we learn that there is some one who attends and cares for your needs. For most of us, our first "love" experiences are with parents – often our mothers. All of us develop an intense attachment with our primary caregivers – most frequently our biological parents. **Attachment theory** tells us that some of our most basic and unconscious emotional responses in intimacy are shaped by the kind of relationship with our parents.

Attachment Styles may take various forms depending on the quality of relationship between the child and mother. If the child experiences sensitive and responsible mothering, the child develops secure attachment style which is appropriate. If there are problems in the relationship the child develops maladaptive styles including avoiding style. The secure attachment style gives child a sense of security and self-worth. It is believed that such adaptive secure attachment style gets transmitted to adolescent and adulthood. Adolescents and adolescent having secure attachment styles are capable of establishing close relationship with others and are capable of sustaining such secure relationship for a longer period of time.

However, some researchers do not agree with this argument. They believe that many events creep into adult's life and may change attachment style induced during childhood years.

4. Resolve Conflicts

Conflict Resolution Style. A great deal of research has focused on how relationship partners deal with conflict and interpret negative behaviours. This is because some amount of conflict is inevitable in our intimate relation. Married couples may encounter differences in their expectations. Differences with respect to spending habits, managing children, arranging higher education for adolescents, and changing own careers may arise. The approaches adopted by intimate partners for solving these problems may strengthen or weaken the relationship.

An interesting inference derived from relationship

research states that *once a relationship is well-established, its success depends more on the absence of conflict (the bad) than on the presence of affection (the good)*. A couple's satisfaction with their marriage is linked significantly more strongly to the level of conflict than it is to the level of positive behaviour. A well-known daily diary study found that a nearly two-thirds of couples' marital satisfaction was related to the occurrence (or lack) of negative behaviours and conflict, and much less to the occurrence (or lack) of positive behaviours. In our intimate relationship the bad seems stronger than the good. A single negative act appears capable of "undoing" countless acts of affection and kindness.

The most extensive studies of marital conflict has been conducted by Gottman. Among his many studies were intensive observation of married couples in the "love lab". This was an apartment set up to video-tape verbal, nonverbal, and physiological responses of couples as they talked about topics posed by the investigator. The topics were controversial and observations were directed to identify strengths and weaknesses.

It was found that negative communication patterns were more predictive of marital satisfaction level and overall relationship quality than were displays of affection and kindness. In particular, these four factors were very harmful

1. *Criticism.* A high proportion of negative as compared to positive comments, remarks and nonverbal signals
2. *Defensiveness.* Taking criticism and comments personally ("I am not going to take it any more")
3. *Stonewalling.* Refusal to respond
4. *Contempt.* Showing scorn, anger, and rejection

Interestingly Gottman wanted to determine the proportion of positive behaviour that neutralizes the effect of a single negative behaviour. On the basis of his observations in "love-lab", a ratio of 5 positive interactions to 1 negative interaction was found to the dividing line between successful and unsuccessful marriages. In a healthy relationship, there are five times more positive than negative interaction. Troubled relationships have very low ratios. The 5-to-1 ratio supports the general principle that 'bad is stronger than good'.

The implication suggests that the harm done by one bad thing needs to be offset by five good things for marriages to be satisfying. The 5-to-1 obviously underlines an approach to improve the quality of relationship – *find ways to reward your partner*. Frequent and simple acts of care, concern, affection and kindness can shift the ratios into the positive range. This makes conflict less likely and easier to resolve when it occurs.

5. Build as many Positives as possible

Capitalization. Positive emotions have beneficial effects that are both independent of and beyond those of negative emotions. In addition to offsetting the ill-effects of negative effect, positive emotions independently enhance the quality of our life. It is just as important to receive supportive responses to our positive life experiences as it is to receive support at the time of our adversity. When people celebrate a positive event (e.g., birth-days felicitation) with others, they derive immense benefits. This process is referred to as **capitalization** (capitalizing on a additional benefits).

In a study, participants kept a daily diary in which they recorded their positive and negative emotions and their life satisfaction. For each day, they also recorded their most important positive event and whether they had shared it with others. Results indicated that on 70% of the days people had shared. It was found that well-being was enhanced on "sharing" days compared to "non-sharing" days.

How do people respond to some positive events (such as promotion, academic achievement, winning a prize) happening to their partners? Research shows four types of reactions in sharing a positive event: (1) *active constructive* (e.g., the person gets the feeling that partner is more happy and excited than person experiencing the event), (2) *active-destructive* (the partner comments on the down side of the event – "you got promotion, but created more enemies for us), (3) *passive-constructive* (the partner says he/she is happy but does not express it enthusiastically), (4) *passive destructive* (the partner does not pay attention to it). The comparison of these four types shows that only active – constructive responses to the sharing of positive life events are related to enhanced relationship. The three other responses types are associated with decreased relationship quality. It clearly posits that capitalization is dependent on an active, enthusiastic, and supporting reaction from one's partner.

6. Use Moderation Approach

Gender-linked Problem Solving Pattern. In the context of positive reactions, researchers have observed a typical gender difference. Women, who are often more attuned to and concerned about the ongoing quality of close relationship, make more demands to resolve problems and to improve a marriage than men. Relationship problems raised by one partner are sensitive issues because they directly or indirectly imply criticism of the other. In raising these issues, women are generally more emotionally expressive and report more intense emotion than men. Men seem generally less sensitive to relationship problems and less comfortable talking about them.

These differences are likely to produce an interaction pattern in which the woman makes demand to talk about a problem and the man withdraws or becomes defensive (refuses to talk). This frustrates the wife and she makes more demand. It is suggested that a balance is needed between these extreme tendencies. The discussion with an attitude of moderation is helpful for enhanced relationship.

7. Adopt Useful Explanation Style

Supportive Explanatory Styles. It is natural that bad (negative) events do happen to one of the two partners. As soon as bad things do happen to one partner, the other hastens to explain it. Who is responsible for the event? It is a fundamental question for which immediate causal explanation is offered. Suppose the husband did not secure promotion. Is it because of his negligence of duty or because of some situational factors?

Generally, it is found that we blame others or external situation when we encounter bad events. But we blame the other person when the other person encounters the problem.

In a healthy relationship, partners should consider the role of external circumstances or situations whole explaining the bad events happening to the partner. "My husband / wife has failed to bring a gift on my birthday not because he or she is inattentive to my emotion, it is because of the current pressure of work". Such an explanatory style of explaining other partner's failure would be helpful in promoting cordial relationship.

Exhibit: Faculty Attribution Style

Success	Failure	
	Internal Factor (Trait / Disposition)	External Factor (Situation / Environment)
Me		
Other	External Factor (Situation / Environment)	Internal Factor (Trait / Disposition)

8. Develop Sense of Humour

Sense of Humour. Humour is a buffer to stress. It has immense role in reducing our stress and providing an outlet for the release of pent-up emotion. In married life, our ability to use humour and diffuse strained communication plays a significant role.

While sexual attraction may decline over years, the strength of humour does not decline. Even 50-year-married couples report that laughing together has made marriage a great success. Humour is undoubtedly one major reason as to why happy couples enjoy each other's company. Humour can detoxify conflict and relieve stress in a relationship.

Laughter is an emotional reaction that most people cannot fake. An obligatory and forced laughter is easily distinguished from the real thing. Because it is less subject to conscious control, a genuine laugh is thought to be an honest expression of how a person really feels.

9. Evolve Commonality of Activity

In many situations, it is possible to develop some activity where partners conjointly do the work. For example, one of the partners may do the secretarial work of the other partner, if possible. The husband and wife can work as doctors in the same unit. One may be the doctor while other is the nurse. By stretching our imagination, we can contemplate various forms of jobs, activities or hobbies where one's work supplements or complements the other's activity. Such a commonality of activity would be a source of combined pleasure.

10. Believe in Relationship Growth

Destiny vrs Growth. People in a relationship may or may not be having similar implicit theories and expectations regarding marriage. There are two distinct implicit theories defined either by a belief in **romantic destiny** or by a belief in **relationship growth**. The basic premise of the romantic destiny theory is that two people are either compatible or they are incompatible. If a marriage runs well, it signals compatibility. If it runs into problem, it indicates incompatibility. "We are right for each other" or "We aren't right for each other" – This is the typical verbal expression of people believing in romantic destiny.

The growth theory assumes that relationships are challenging and will grow and develop over time. People believing in growth theory feel that obstacles foster development. They assume that obstacles and difficulties in relationship are but natural. Yet partners have the ability to overcome obstacles and to intensify the bonding.

People who hold to the romantic destiny theory endorse items such as, "A successful relationship is mostly a matter of finding a compatible partner right from the start", and "Early troubles in a relationship signify a poor match between partners". Growth theory advocates would agree with items such as, "Challenges and obstacles in a relationship can make love even stronger", or "It takes a lot of time and effort to cultivate a good relationship".

A strong belief in romantic destiny leads to an interpretation of conflict as a sign of incompatibility over which couples can exercise little control. A belief in relationship growth provides a more positive and accepting perspective on the inevitable conflict. From a growth perspective, conflict is a natural part of all relationships and it does not mean that someone has to be at fault. Problems are temporary and solvable. Hence, effort and commitment can make the difference between success and failure.

In sum, the main ingredients of happy couple life include friendship and commitment. Deep and abiding friendship is the top reason of lasting marriages. Both partners agree: "My spouse is my best friend". In addition, couples recognize the importance of strong commitment to making their relationship truly permanent. "Together we laugh" – This is an off-quoted voice of happy couples.

Know Your Explanatory Style

You are given a number of events. Imagine each event happening to you. Each event is followed by two alternative explanations: A & B. Choose the explanation that you consider appropriate for you.

1. Your spouse/ intimate friend forgot to bring you a gift on your birthday.
   A. She / he was neglectful
   B. She / he was under pressure of work.
2. Your spouse / intimate friend did not congratulate you on your promotion
   A. She / he was careless
   B. She / he was too busy with domestic responsibility
3. Your spouse / intimate friend failed to pick you up at the Railway Station

A. She / he faced formidable traffic jam

B. She / he chatted with her / his friend so long that she / he lost track of time

4. Your spouse / intimate friend did not give you medicine in time

   A. She / he was unmindful

   B. Children forced her / him to pay attention to their needs.

5. Your spouse / intimate friend picked up a quarrel with you

   A. She / he is quarrelsome

   B. She / he was in angry mood that day

6. Your spouse / intimate friend spoiled your dress while ironing it

   A. She / he is always uncaring

   B. She / he was very tired then

7. Your spouse / intimate friend spoke rudely

   A. She / he is impolite

   B. She / he was in a bad mood that time

8. Your spouse / intimate friend told you a lie

   A. She / he is very casual

   B. She / he wanted to save herself / himself from your anger that time

9. Your spouse / intimate friend could not complete the work

   A. She / he is incompetent

   B. She / he is not skilled in the work she / he was doing

10. Your spouse / intimate friend failed to arrange the function in time

    A. She / he lacks in skill

    B. She / he is poor in organizing event

11. Your spouse / intimate friend played a game but lost miserably

A. She / he has no ability

B. She / he is weak in the game she / he play

12. Your spouse / intimate friend went out for shopping, but bought useless things

    A. She / he lacks in intelligence

    B. She / he is poor in money matters

13. Your spouse / intimate friend cooked delicious food for you

    A. She / he is competent in cooking

    B. She / he received cooperation from all family members

14. Your spouse / intimate friend told a joke and everybody laughed

    A. She / he told the joke properly

    B. Everybody was in humorous mood

15. Your spouse / intimate friend accomplished success

    A. She / he is versatile

    B. People extended support

16. Your spouse / intimate friend did a good project

    A. She / he has ability

    B. Luck favoured her / him a lot

17. Your spouse / intimate friend contested for a post and won

    A. She / he is popular

    B. Things worked out finely that occasion

18. Your spouse / intimate friend delivered a nice speech

    A. She / he is usually well-spoken

    B. People were in a mood to appreciate that day

19. Your spouse / intimate friend solved a problem

    A. She / he is always intelligent

    B. Others were helpful in extending solutions that time

20. Your spouse / intimate friend defended her / his position well

A. She / he is usually knowledgeable

B. People supported her / him during the debate

21.	Your spouse / intimate friend invested money did got good returns

A. She / he is skillful

B. She / he is good in monetary matters

22.	Your spouse / intimate friend played tennis and won

A. She / he is good in games

B. She / he is good in tennis

23.	Your spouse / intimate friend chose the right school for your children

A. She / he is insightful

B. She / he is judicious with respect to children's education

24.	Your spouse / intimate friend was appreciated for her / his work

A. She / he is a deserving person

B. She / he is good in the work she / he did

Interpretation

- Count the number of B's from item 1 through 12 and the number of A's from item 13 through 24.
- Add these two scores
- This is your adaptive (good) explanatory style score
- Interpret as indicated

  below 6: poor relationship

  7 to 12 : fair relationship

  13 to 18 : good relationship

  more than 19 : very good relationship

Chapter : 26

Train Your Brain

For decades' brain science held as given that the central nervous system did not generate new neurons. Every students of neuroscience was taught this proposition. But this unshakable dogma was shattered in the late 1990's, largely through research in molecular biology at the cellular level.

The finding – that the brain and nervous system generate new cells as learning or repeated experiences dictate – has put the theme of plasticity at the front and center of neuroscience. It is believed that neural plasticity – the brain's ability to reshape as experience moulds it – will psychology itself in coming years.

What is damaging to brain and behavior is the destructive emotion. Some antidotes to such destructive emotion can be conceptualized in neuroscientific terms. One of the ways to think about antidotes to destructive emotion is by facilitating the activation of the regions of the frontal lobe that suppress or moderate the activity of the amygdale. The amygdale has been shown to be very important for certain kinds of negative emotions. It is also known that specific regions of the frontal lobe reduce the activity of the amygdale. Through this mechanism we can change the brain so that a person will show less negative and more positive emotions.

Paul Ekman uses the phrase "refractory period" for when the emotion is very difficult to stop once it is initiated. A person is not receptive to new information while in the grip of negative emotion. One possibility is that the cultivation of certain skills many facilitate the disruption of the automatic negative emotion. That would give a person an opportunity to pause and shorten the refractory period – and to become more conscious that initial moment of the arising of the emotion so that it can be cut off before the negative effects occur.

Diagram of Brain with Amygdala

Since it is possible to cultivate positive affects, these could be a direct antidote to the experience of certain kinds of negative emotions. *What is the mechanism that allows these kinds of antidotes to work?*

The diagram shows the key areas in the frontal lobe. The medial portion, the deep down in the lobe, is the area most heavily interconnected with the amygdale. The amygdale is the area that is closely related to the negative qualities of experiences such as depression. This is more active in people who are depressed. It is more active in people who have posttraumatic stress disorder. It is more active in people who are more anxious. The medial area of the frontal cortex plays an inhibitory role. When this area becomes more active, the amygdale shows a decrease in activation. People differ in their temperament in the extent to which these areas of the prefrontal cortex are active and the amygdale is correspondingly underactive.

A number of neuroscientists have searched through the entire brain to see what area is most strongly associated with a person's reports of positive emotions and decrease in the destructive emotion. They find the same area most strongly associated with decrease in amygdale activation. So the question then is, how can we strengthen this area that inhibits the amygdale so that we can increase a person's positive emotions and decrease the negative emotions?

Something very interesting and exciting has emerged from experimental research of Professor Richard Davidson (Madison, USA). Davidson recorded the brain activity of meditators and other people. Davidson found that the stronger the leftward tilt in prefrontal activity the more positive emotion in their daily life people reported. In earlier research, Davidson found that people who show the distinctive leftward prefrontal tilt in brain activity associated with the positive emotions also have a more robust activity on some parameters of immune function.

The distribution of the rates of left-to-right prefrontal activity is a critical parameter. Negative emotions activate the right prefrontal area, positive the left. The ratio of the two predicts the range of moods a person is likely to feel day to day.

Finally, it is most important to recognize that meditation is the process that increases leftward prefrontal activity. This has been evinced through the case analyses of meditators as well as controlled experimental methods.

Ordinarily, our emotions come to us as our life conditions change, shifting for better or worse. But meditation practitioners gradually develop inner locus for their emotional states, an equanimity less vulnerable to life's ups and downs. Gradually the meditators' moods are governed more by an inner reality rather than by outer events. *Sukha* is the Sanskrit term for this sense of repleteness, of an inner contentment and calm joy that abides regardless of external circumstances. *Sukha* differs from ordinary happiness or pleasure, which typically depends on what happens to us. In this respect, *sukha* seems to reflect that leftward frontal tilt.

It offers a positive psychology, a model of human development that goes beyond the prevailing theories of the West (concerning well-being).

Points to Ponder

1. It is possible to rewire brain through meditation
2. Amygdale is associated with activation of negative thoughts
3. Increased activity in prefrontal area of the brain is associated with positive thoughts and decreased activity of amygdale
4. Leftward prefrontal tilt is the mechanism that increases positive emotions and decreases negative thoughts
5. Regular meditation is the surer path for leftward prefrontal tilt.

Chapter : 27

Management of Thought, Emotion and Time

Thinking may be viewed as a cognitive process characterized by the use of symbols as representations of objects or events. When we walk along the road, we do not necessarily engage in thought (although, of course, we may), but if we refer to walking that is not now going on, then we must use a symbolic reference. A *symbol* is anything that stands for or refers to something other than itself. The word 'book' stands for printed pages with a firm cover- the object called book – but of course the symbol 'book is not the book. Such a symbolic reference characterizes thought. Thoughts can deal with remembered, absent or imagined objects, and events, as well as with those currently impinging on the sensory system.

Nature of the Thought Process

The basic elements of thought involve concepts, propositions and images. Concepts are mental categories for objects, events or experiences. which are similar to one another in one or more respects. Propositions are sentences that relate one concept to another. Images are the mental pictures of the world.

Thought and imagination differ from each other in one essential manner. Thought is goal-directed whereas imagination is without specific goals. Fantasy, daydreams and reverie are several forms of imagination. From this standpoint, thinking involves decision-making. Furthermore, decision requires a two-stage process. In the first stage, the individual goes for reasoning and in the second phase, the individual comes to the conclusion and adopts a decision.

Reasoning involves transforming available information in order to reach specific conclusions. Formal reasoning derives conclusions from specific premises. In contrast, everyday reasoning is less clear-cut and more complex. Reasoning is subject to several forms of error and bias. It can be distorted by our emotions and/or beliefs; by our tendency to focus primarily on evidence that confirms our beliefs, or confirmation bias and by our tendency to assume that we could have predicted actual events more successfully than is really the case, or the hindsight effect.

Another important aspect concerning thought relates to its relationship with language. Thought and language are intimately connected. It is important to recognize that language represents a system of symbols. It has been observed that cultural context in general and language in particular influence human behaviour. For example, Arabs do have a large number of words to denote different types of camels. Consequently, they can discriminate camels more accurately than other people.

Human Values and Thought Process
As pointed out earlier, human thinking is guided by symbols which are transmitted by the socio-cultural system. If a specific socio-cultural system attaches priority to certain

elements, people would have greater inclination to think about those objects and events. Sorokin, a great sociologist, makes a distinction between sensate society and spiritual society. In sensate society, people attach priorities to objects and events that are connected with sensory gratification. On the contrary, spiritual society attaches importance to values and meanings.

The foregoing argument suggests that human thought process in influenced both by genetic memory and the societal climate. Hence it is argued that the creation of a value-oriented cultural climate would induce on inclination to think in terms of human values.

Strategies for Value-guided Thoughts

Since thinking is a symbolic activity, any attempt to change the content and direction of thought process has to be undertaken very carefully. Although several strategies can be suggested to guide values oriented thought, a number of major guidelines are suggested.

Distinction between the thought and the thinker. In many situations, thinking brings problems primarily because individuals do not perceive the difference between the thought and the thinker. It is important to recognize that objects do not cause problem. For example, the rich food in the restaurant is not a cause for the problem. But problem begins when the individual thinks to grab the food and eats it. The fundamental point causing the problem involves our association with the object. If we build faulty relationship with the object, the thought of this relationship becomes the root of the problem. In other words, we need to develop right kind of association with the object. Here, we make a distinction between an information and a command. Information is more or less neutral but when we give it a command form, problem begins to creep in. For instance, the information may include the thought. Puri is a nice place. But we get into problematic thought when we develop slavery to the command: we must go to Puri.

Positive thinking. It has been observed that depressive individuals think of negative memories. They turn their attention to the darker sides of their lives. It needs no argument to convince people that positive thinking is very helpful in the management of our personal lives.

Substitute thoughts. It has been observed that negative thoughts overpower the individual. Fighting against the negative thought may not be a successful exercise. When an individual fights against a negative thought (say, fear), the negative thought such as fear becomes more powerful. Therefore, it is more useful to avoid fighting and adopt an alternative (substitute) activity. For example, an individual may not be successful to become a vegetarian, if he goes on fighting against the ideas of taking meat or fish. On the contrary, the person will be successful if he or she develops liking for vegetarian food such as milk and fruits.

Taking responsibility. In many situations, people feel helpless to control their thoughts. They rationalize that their negative thoughts are product of the situations in which they have been placed. However, this is not a logical argument. A child cannot create his or her own environment. It the child enters into a depressive setting, the child ought to be depressive. On the contrary, an adult can change the texture of a situation. The adult must recognize the fact that he or she is responsible for his or her thoughts and moods. Such a recognition of his or her responsibility would be helpful in managing thought.

Relationship Between Thought and Emotions

An adequate understanding of the relationship between thought and emotion requires the knowledge regarding an important piece of scientific information. Psychologists, neurologists and neuropsychiartists have conclusively shown that our feeling brain is older than the thinking brain. In the evolutionary process, the feeling brain was formed first. Subsequently the thinking brain was formed. Although the human brain is structurally one, it has two functional parts: thinking function and feeling function. This implies that feeling and emotion are older and they have important place in the management of the human life. Furthermore, emotions are stronger than thoughts. Even the word emotion is derived from the expression enhancing motion.

Prior to discussing the strategies for the management of emotions, its nature can briefly be stated. Emotions have physiological correlates. This has an important implication. For instance, if we see a snake and run, we experience fear. If we hit a snake we may feel aggressive. In other wards, an emotion produces a specific bodily reaction. If we change the bodily reaction, we may also change the emotion. Secondly, emotions have emergency functions. During emotions, normal activities such as digestion is temporarily suspended. The surplus energy is spent to deal with the emergency. Finally, our emotion can be both positive and negative. Positive emotions such as love and affection have constructive values. On the contrary, negative emotions such as fear, anxiety and sadness have destructive properties.

Strategies for Controlling Emotions

Although emotional control is not easy, but constant learning and practice helps the individuals to manage emotions in a constructive manner. A number of strategies can be suggested in this context.

Using emotional intelligence. Recently psychologists have advised to develop our emotional intelligence. Previously people were talking about intelligence quotient (IQ) while telling about human success. Now the scenario has been changed. Psychologists have led us to believe that we need to develop emotional quotient (EQ). Emotional Intelligence includes self-awareness, interpersonal sensitivity, self-motivation, self-control and positive mood. In other words, we must attach priority to the development of our feeling resources. Once we develop emotional intelligence, we would have smooth and happy relationship with others.

Adopting positive body postures. It is a common believe that our moods produce corresponding body postures. When we are depressed, we sit in a particular way. When we are happy, we work briskly. When we are cheerful, we smile. These statements express the relationship between our moods and our bodily postures. However, it is to be remembered that it could be the other way. Our bodily posture may also change our emotion. When we work briskly, we are likely to feel smart (not depressed). When we smile we feel cheerful. Thus, it is possible to adopt right kind of bodily postures and physical activities so that appropriate moods would be generated.

Sublimation. An effective strategy to deal with negative emotion involves the method of sublimation. Sublimation implies channelizing negative emotions in a constructive manner. For instance, a person's aggressiveness can be redirected towards physical act of gardening and beautifying the surroundings. Similarly, a person experiencing the frustration may channelize his or her emotion for creative works such as art, literature and painting.

Need of Time Management

Management of time and achieving goals constitute a formidable challenge. Both these objectives are interrelated. An individual has to develop skills in a planned manner.

One has to understand that there are two important dimensions of time management urgency and importance. Generally, people strive a lot to work on agenda which are urgent and highly important. Important works where urgency is not attached get neglected. Hence an important pointer is to shift important and low urgency activities to important and high urgency cell.

Urgency

	Low	High
High		
Low		

Importance

Strategies for Time Management

The concept of economics says, we need to manage and plan because our resources are limited. The four important resources at our disposal are

1. Man
2. Money
3. Machinery
4. Material

But most of us forget besides these resources one most important resource is time, which we always fall short of. Otherwise, people would not resent standing or sitting in queue. If we manage our time properly then we can increase our output in a given time by many folds. But question is what is managing time?

The practice of ensuring that the effort and time spent during normal working day is allocated to the agreed objectives and priorities of the work is management of time.

Self-Audit. We need to plan out time because we are never sufficient of it. Great Einstein even after so much contribution lamented in his last days: "Alas I had more time."

In order to gain control of your time, first, you must ask yourself these three basic questions.

i)   How have I been using my time?
ii)   How am I wasting my time?
iii)   How can I make better use of my time in the future?

By answering first question you can divide your time in these categories.

i)   Time you are devoting to your duties.
ii)   Time devoted to your friends, known person etc.
iii)   Home time

Surprisingly most of us will find that we devote not more than 15% of our total time on our duty. The duty occupies less than 1/6th of our total time. Even if we increase it marginally the result will be fantastic.

Reducing wasteful habits. The next thing we must concentrate on is how do we waste our time. Most of us have developed our own time wasting techniques! We have become so used to them that hardly we realize how much harm we are doing to the nation, our institutions and to ourselves. Some of favorite time wasting techniques are following.

When we are not effective in communication (i.e. using proper language, words and the order of the ideas), we take much more time in explaining our position. Poor communication can result in misunderstanding. The other person leaves the scene what he thinks you said or told to him whereas you think you told something else. The result is that the same person will come to your seeking same information again; quite likely he will tend to quarrel with you. Both of you will try to explain your own language resulting in wasting lot of time.

Knowing the duty well will save a lot of time for you. If you know your duty well, then you can work much faster resulting in saving lot of time. If you don't know your duty, you will tend to beat about the bush. It has been seen that the expert is able to explain even the most difficult thing in simplest language and shortest period. Not knowing the duty may trigger for some unnecessary arguments as well.

Sometimes we waste our time in unnecessary arguments even when we are good communicator and know our duty well. This is due to our ego. Remember: in such cases, you must make transaction with other people with a sense of maturity. Non-Planning is also a big time wasting technique. We must plan before we start doing our work. Gossip Kills a lot of time. Some known person comes and we have the tendency to leave our position at the cost of many people waiting for our service. Teasession in our institutions are quite popular. Every one of us know the harmful effects of these tea session not only on our productivity but also on our health; Yet, we fail to control them as each one of us is conformist by nature and conform to anything what the others or society does. Tea-session can be useful provided they are one or maximum two in a day.

Most of us are infested with monkey habits. What is this habit? So and so is doing that much work, therefore, I shall also not do more than that. If this is not monkey habit then, what is this? We are behaving like monkeys. Even, at the cost of running the risk of becoming slow in our life we are infested with this habit. As human being we should copy the good point of other and not everything good and bad. You must have heard the story of the cap-seller and the monkeys. Let us leave our monkey habits and behave like human beings.

Effective Use of Time

The third question is how to make better use of time. In this regard we must remember the above discussed time wasting techniques and strive to avoid them. For sake of revision we summarize them.

1. **Use your communication skills effectively.**
2. Know your duty well.
3. Plan your work.
4. Avoid unnecessary argument.
5. Use tea session constructively.

Achieving goals. The goal of achieving target can be given tangible reality by systematic psychological and behavioural changes. The following sequence of activities are important in this direction.

Avoid planning fallacy. Planning is necessary for achieving targets, but many persons commit *planning* *fallacy*, they under-estimate the amount of time required for a goal. When they look at the future, they forget all about the past. It is necessary to have a correct estimate of required time. Repeated failures reduce self-confidence. Hence, it is necessary to have a realistic planning and avoid planning fallacy.

Boost your self-confidence. Skill is necessary for success, but it is also necessary to have self-confidence to execute a function competently. Self-confidence is a belief-system. Self –confidence can be developed by broadening the field of exposure, by undertaking moderately difficult works initially (there by increasing the possibility of initial success), and observing right kind of *role models.* This is very important.

Construct tangible targets: Constructing tangible targets is very helpful. Ambiguous and conceptual goals generate complexity. Even there is a broad super ordinate (conceptual) goal, it must be broken into small tangible goals. Goals must be quantified. It helps in the pursuit of goals.

Develop proximal (near) goals. While fixing goals, it is useful to set near goals. Suppose an individual desires to collect Rs. 100, 00000 as loan repayment in a year. Although this goal is set, it is helpful to convert the target into monthly targets (Rs. 10, 00000 per month). A near goal appears to be easy to be pursued.

Enhance self-motivation: In order to enhance self-motivation, it is necessary to link the activity with out-come or values. For instance, if one values others' appreciation, one has to persuade himself/herself that achieving target is *essential* for securing appreciation.

Chapter : 28

Meaningfulness in Life

The experience of meaningfulness in life is vital to human existence. This experience has a large number of benefits. It is associated with higher quality of life. It is linked with superior self reported health, decreased mortality, slower age-related cognitive decline, and lower incidence of psychological disorder. Those who report their live as meaningful are more likely to rely on adaptive coping strategies. In the work domain, meaning in life is related to heightened occupational adjustment. In the social domain, those who rate their lives as quite meaningful are rated by other as more socially appealing.

Yet, life reveals a paradox. The meaning in life appears to be hotly sought after and at times lacking in people's lives. Whether it is a rare commodity or a common place can be answered later. Let us first conceptualize the concept. While a number of diverse definitions of meaning in life have been offered, there are atleast three common themes. First, a meaningful life is one that a sense of purpose. *Meaning in life* and *purpose in life* are often interchangeably used. Second, a meaningful life is one possesses *significance*. Third, the meaningful life makes sense to the person living it, it is comprehensible, and it is characterized by regularity, predictability, or reliable connections. Lives may be experienced as meaningful when they are felt to have a significance beyond the trivial or momentary, to have purpose, or to have coherence that transcends chaos. Meaning is the web of connections, understandings, and interpretations that help us comprehend our experience and formulate plans directing our energies to the achievement of our desired future. Meaning provide us with the sense that our lives matter, and they make sense, and that they are more than the sum of our seconds, days, and years.

Instead of debating over the issue of siaraty versus abundance of meaning in life, it is wiser to identify the foundational sources. *Social relationship* appears to be a potent source. Individuals,who are lonely, socially excluded, ignored, or ostracized are worse off. Those who are included are well off. *Essentially, social exclusion reliably leads to lower ratings by meaningful existence.* Those who receive rejecting feedback lower their self-ratings on meaningfulness. **When we are socially connected, life fees more meaningful.**

Positive mood is another powerful source. Positive mood or positive affect refers to the experience of mild pleasant feelings: the extent to which a person is happy, pleased, cheerful, or experiencing enjoyment. **Meaning in life is consistently positively correlated with positive affect.** There are various mood induction techniques. Even mild experiences that enhance positive affect (e.g., listening to happy music or reading the funnies) can promoting a sense of meaning in life. Thus, positive mood is not simply an outcome of meaning in life; the causal arrow goes in the other direction as well. When we are in a good mood, the life feels more meaningful.

More recently, psychological research has shown that meaning in life is sensitive to the presence of reliable patterns or coherence in environment stimuli. Drawing on the cognitive component of meaning in life, it is found that perception of meaning is stronger after an experience with stimuli characterized by pattern or coherence. Stated simply, when stimuli make sense, life is more meaningful.

In one study, participants viewed a series of pictures of trees. The 16 photos included four for each of the four seasons. The participants thought their job was to evaluate the contrast in the picture. The investigator systematically varied the order of the pictures. In one group, the 16 pictures appeared in a random order. In another, they were arranged so that they followed the change in seasons, over four cycles (conforming to spring, summer, autumn, and winter). After completing the rating task, all participants rated their meaning in life. It was shown that meaning in life was rated significantly higher in the seasonal pattern group than in the random group.

In sum, the experience of meaning in life can be augmented by way of forming social bonds, seeking positive effects and encountering patterned (coherent) stimuli in the environment.

Points to Ponder
1. Meaning in life is essential to our survival.
2. Enhance this experience by way of
   A. Affect: Seek more and more positive affects
   B. Binding: Form social bonding (social inclusion)
   C. Coherence: Discover pattern or coherence in stimuli

About the Book

- The book is the first of this time to deal with employee counselling.
- It provides a tool box for service providers working in employee's assistant centers.
- It offers basic models (both classical and contemporary) of counselling.
- Useful for organizational development and renewal process
- Serves as a guide for general leaders in their life transactions
- A navigator's compass to deal with employees' problems
- A must-reading for promising leaders

Black Eagle Books

www.blackeaglebooks.org
info@blackeaglebooks.org

Black Eagle Books, an independent publisher, was founded
as a nonprofit organization in April, 2019. It is our mission
to connect and engage the Indian diaspora and the world at
large with the best of works of world literature published
on a collaborative platform, with special emphasis on
foregrounding Contemporary Classics and New Writing.

www.ingramcontent.com/pod-product-compliance
Lightning Source LLC
Chambersburg PA
CBHW030502210326
41597CB00013B/764